"This book invites each of us into a supernatural transformation to conformity to the image of Christ. I believe everyone in the world deserves to have an encounter with a God that looks just like Jesus. This book is a guide for you to take your desire and move into your destiny. It is an honor for me to have a friend like Putty Putman who is living and loving from the heart of Jesus. A new Jesus movement has come to show how good the Father is. Invest in the Christ in you that is the hope for the world around you!"

Leif Hetland, president, Global Mission Awareness;
author, *Giant Slayers*

"*Live Like Jesus* puts excitement back into the lives of believers who are feeling bored and unsatisfied in their walk with God. Putty Putman addresses the very real feelings that Christians face of wanting the 'more' of God that is displayed in the Bible but simply not knowing how to get there. He unearths the real meaning of the normal Christian life and teaches us how to walk in our divine mandate as world-changers and history-makers. In this book Putty pastors readers through a journey that he himself went on, breaking the boxes that religion has tried to squeeze God into, and demonstrating just how powerful and exhilarating the Gospel is."

Kris Vallotton, senior associate leader, Bethel Church,
Redding, California; co-founder, Bethel School
of Supernatural Ministry; author, *The Supernatural Ways
of Royalty* and *Destined to Win*

"It is easy to fully endorse this revelatory, life-changing book because Putty actually lives like Jesus! As his senior pastor, I have observed Putty's life as a husband, father, teacher and lover of Jesus. The Holy Spirit has trusted him with some powerful

truths that will inspire, challenge and excite you to live like Jesus!"

Dianne Leman, senior pastor, The Vineyard Church
of Central Illinois

"Putty Putman's *Live Like Jesus* challenges Christians to live supernatural lives—something I believe true biblical discipleship requires. I know Putty personally and can vouch for his commitment to Christ, and I can vouch that this book is based not on theory, but on practice."

Dr. Randy Clark, Apostolic Network of Global Awakening

"Believers, the Gospel inside you is bigger than you know. God in you is bigger than you know! Aren't you ready to know? If you want everyone who encounters you to encounter Jesus, you've got to first encounter His full Gospel. Let my brilliant friend Putty show you how to live like Jesus."

Laura Harris Smith, C.N.C., author, *The 30-Day Faith Detox*
and *Seeing the Voice of God*

LIVE
LIKE
JESUS

LIVE LIKE JESUS

DISCOVER THE POWER AND IMPACT
OF YOUR TRUE IDENTITY

PUTTY PUTMAN

Chosen

a division of Baker Publishing Group
Minneapolis, Minnesota

© 2017 by Rob Putman

Published by Chosen Books
11400 Hampshire Avenue South
Bloomington, Minnesota 55438
www.chosenbooks.com

Chosen Books is a division of
Baker Publishing Group, Grand Rapids, Michigan

Printed in the United States of America

Library of Congress Control Number: 2017946304

ISBN 978-0-8007-9852-9

Unless otherwise indicated, Scripture quotations are from The Holy Bible, English Standard Version® (ESV®), copyright © 2001 by Crossway, a publishing ministry of Good News Publishers. Used by permission. All rights reserved. ESV Text Edition: 2011

Scripture quotations identified NIV are from the Holy Bible, New International Version®. NIV®. Copyright © 1973, 1978, 1984, 2011 by Biblica, Inc.™ Used by permission of Zondervan. All rights reserved worldwide. www.zondervan.com

Cover design by Studio Gearbox

17 18 19 20 21 22 23   7 6 5 4 3 2 1

In keeping with biblical principles of creation stewardship, Baker Publishing Group advocates the responsible use of our natural resources. As a member of the Green Press Initiative, our company uses recycled paper when possible. The text paper of this book is composed in part of post-consumer waste.

To Jesus, the author and perfecter of our faith,
and to my wife, Brittany, for being willing
to take this crazy journey with me.

///////////////////////////////////////

Contents

Foreword

About seven years ago, my then regional overseer in the Vineyard movement asked me to come and meet a young Ph.D. grad who was in his church and interested in the practical work of the Kingdom. He introduced me to Rob (Putty) Putman. Now, at that time, many people were asking me for interviews and ways to gain a better understanding of becoming practitioners of Kingdom ministry. I always assumed they were curious and dabbling. With Putty, it felt different. As you read this book, you will see what I mean. Putty is a gifted teacher.

Putty is deep and gifted at raising people up to understand the truth of the Kingdom. *Live Like Jesus* explores some of the hard questions we have all been asking (or have not realized we have been asking). Putty challenges us to step beyond what we have concluded or been told in order to see the work Christ has done and the life we are meant to live. You will see this early on, starting in chapter 2, his chapter on "The Gospel I Thought I Knew."

Chapter 4, which discusses "The True Gospel" and how Jesus destroyed the works of the devil, is near to my heart, as I dealt with this subject in my first book. Putty shares a side to this subject that will invite you to make this your life's work.

I could go on, but you need to explore this one for yourself.

As you read *Live Like Jesus*, you will be challenged and called higher to the realities that await us in this life of righteousness and true identity. Be prepared to be stretched and increased to live a life in the Kingdom that started and ends in deep relationship with the Father.

Loosen your belt, 'cause it is a full-meal deal. Then tighten your seat belt, 'cause it is quite a ride.

Robby Dawkins, international speaker
and ministry equipper; author, *Do What Jesus Did*

Acknowledgments

Creating a book is a large undertaking, and it is not a solo project. Many contributed to this book, in one way or another, and it would not have been possible without them all.

To my family: Brittany and the kids, thanks for being willing to give me up for all those blocks of time I spent writing and editing. They are coming to something at last! Dad, thanks for passing along a passion for the written word and for dreaming with me about publishing.

To my Vineyard family: Thank you for the journey of the last several years. It has been more exciting and adventuresome than I would have imagined. It is wonderful to be part of a community that continually presses in for everything God has for us. Hap and Di, thanks for modeling so many things incredibly for me: passion for following Jesus, leadership, learning, risk-taking and more. This would not be possible if you had not believed in me.

To the SoKM team and students: Thanks for pushing the envelope. The Lord has so many incredible things on the horizon for us. I love heading toward the future together. The breakthroughs of the present and future will be more than worth the price we have paid to get there.

To the Chosen team: Thanks for taking a risk on my young voice. It has been a tremendous honor and a lot of fun to work with you. You have made this whole thing possible, and it has been a joy along the way.

There are doubtless many more I am sure I have forgotten. Thank you to each and every person who has been a part of this journey and who has held me up, one way or another. I could not have done it without you.

1

Welcome to the Journey

Linda had been a Christian for years, and she felt frustrated with God. She attended church every weekend unless an emergency interfered. She did everything she could to have the kind of relationship with God she believed was possible.

A wife and mother of two young sons, she and her husband had met years before, in college at a campus ministry. Ever since that time, more than anything else, Linda wanted to know what it was to be close to God. Her pastor shared about the value of reading Scripture and about personal devotion to Jesus, but something just never seemed to click. Every time she sat down to read the Bible, she found it confusing. Every time she reached toward God in prayer, she believed her words never went farther than the ceiling. She desperately wanted the *personal* in her "personal Lord and Savior," but she could not seem to find it. God felt distant and confusing. She understood Him as an idea but could not find any relational connection with Him.

Steve was a rather successful businessman. He found out early in his career he had a knack for market positioning, and his recommendations often helped his employer, a software production company, increase their revenue by noticeable amounts. Over the course of several years, he advanced in his career to become the vice president of marketing and was doing quite well for himself. Along the way, a neighbor invited him to church, where he met and gave his life to Jesus.

Steve loved God and wanted to follow Him wholeheartedly, but he struggled to overcome a habit he had long fallen prey to: pornography. His battle with pornography had cycled on and off for more than two decades. He went long stretches living above it, but when situations provoked him to unusual anxiety, he ended up turning to porn to manage the anxiety for weeks at a time. He tried everything he could to get traction toward quitting, but nothing seemed to make a difference.

This weekend, Steve was traveling for work again. As the day dragged on, he noticed he was wrestling with the knowledge that at the end of the night, he would go back to his hotel room, where a television with multiple channels presented him with ripe opportunities to fall off the wagon again. He felt tired and weak—something he knew had caused trouble before. It would be a long trip . . .

Jackie had recently given her life to Jesus. She experienced a profound sense of purpose from her newfound faith and church family. Every day seemed fresh, and life was rich with possibilities. But as she began to experience a life lived with Jesus, she discovered she had difficulty wrapping her heart around the idea that she was fully forgiven. She had a rather checkered past before coming to know Jesus—one filled with experimentation with drugs, sex and other vices. In an effort to find meaning, she had explored Buddhist meditation, along with a smattering of other non-Christian religious practices. Her parents were very moral and had instilled in her a strong sense of right and wrong. She wrestled with deep guilt, shame and regret for her prior choices. She knew she was supposed to be forgiven, but she did not seem to be experiencing that forgiveness. Why was it that after receiving the forgiveness Jesus offered her, she still felt as guilty as ever?

Phil and his wife, Sarah, had enjoyed a relatively positive marriage for the last 22 years. While they never had children, due to infertility, they were a good fit for each other, and the strong commitment they both felt toward Jesus and their church community cemented their life together.

Late one evening, their next-door neighbor, Angela, knocked on their door. As they welcomed her in, she was crying and shaking. They helped her calm down and asked her to explain what was happening.

"We got in a fight, and he finally decided he was leaving me . . . ," she uttered between sobs.

Phil and Sarah knew Angela and Todd had been living together for the last three years and had married each other about six months prior when they discovered Angela was pregnant. Phil and Sarah sat there, uncertain how to proceed. They knew Jesus had given them a strong marriage, and they wished for some way to share that gift with others, but they had no idea where to start. In a flash, it became clear: They knew their faith should be able to bring real answers to the crises around them every day, but they did not know how that worked when the rubber hit the road.

Is Our Faith the Real Deal?

As a pastor, I encounter people with stories similar to these on a regular basis. Unfortunately, they resonate with many of us more than we would like. While we may be committed to Jesus and the message of the Gospel, if we are honest with ourselves, we have some pretty serious struggles living the kind of life we see portrayed and promised in Scripture. We struggle with anger, fear, worry, lust, lying and the like. We feel pushed back and forth by our circumstances, or God feels distant. We begin to realize our faith consists more of a set of ideas than a real relationship with God, and when we bump into opportunities to share what God has given us, we often do not know how.

I would like to challenge you to do a reality check: Is this where you are? How satisfied are you with your Christian experience? Does it satisfy you, or do you feel like you are going through the motions? Do you feel content or frustrated? Fulfilled or lacking? Do not give me the religious-positivity answer. Be gut-wrenchingly honest. Is your faith everything to you that it seems like it should be?

What if I told you the part of you that feels like life is supposed to be thrilling and vibrant might be the Holy Spirit inside you, trying to move you to more? Many of us live with a gnawing sense that *there must be more to this whole Christianity thing than what I'm living*, but we cannot seem to find it. We stumble around and struggle to see how our faith is applicable, let alone exciting. At best, many of us live with a sense of discontent. At worst, we resign ourselves to a "this will have to do" posture toward our walk with God. We know it is the Good News, but if we are honest, it does not always feel all that good.

The issue usually is not our heart posture. More than anything, we want a life characterized by a rich and full relationship with God. We want our lives to be submitted to His purpose and to live in victory over sin. We want to represent Him faithfully in the opportunities we have. We love Jesus and want these things, but it seems difficult to get there. At the very least, it can feel like a three-steps-forward, two-steps-backward kind of experience. If the life we believe is possible is not completely out of reach, it requires at least a tremendous process to get there.

Then, when we hit the point where we stop pretending this treadmill of faith is somehow satisfying us, we often turn our doubts inward: *What if there's something wrong with me? I must be a pretty lousy Christian. Maybe I'm not trying hard enough. Am I really taking this seriously?* These conversations with ourselves usually only convince us to try harder and to beat ourselves up more when we fail—which does not help much.

Eventually, even the promises of Scripture seem illusory. "His yoke is easy, His burden is light" must apply to everyone else, we figure. "More than conquerors" does not describe us, and being a "light to the world" will have to be handled by the rest of the Church. We resolve ourselves to a faith we feel is barely enough to get us by.

Yet there is a deep part of us that knows it is not supposed to be like this. We may not be able to find the road forward for ourselves, but we know, somehow, there is one. Our lives must be able to be richer and fuller than they are. And that is what makes the situation all the more frustrating. We hang on to faith in a better future, but we resign ourselves to the hopeless belief that there is no road we can find to get there.

Here is what Paul says about our life in Christ:

> For the death he died he died to sin, once for all, but the life he lives he lives to God. So you also must consider yourselves dead to sin and alive to God in Christ Jesus.
>
> Romans 6:10–11

Paul exhorts us that inasmuch as Jesus died to sin, we are to see ourselves that much dead to sin, and the extent to which He is alive to God is the same extent we are. We are dead to sin and alive to God if we are in Christ Jesus—yet if we are honest, most of us feel like the opposite is true: We are alive to sin and dead to God. God feels distant, even unreal, but sin creeps into our experience all the time.

I want to be clear about this: *It does not have to be this way.* Paul points us to a reality that can be ours. The Bible is not lying when it invites us to the promises it proclaims. But the answer to getting there is not found in continuing to try harder to do what is not working. If we do not experience ourselves as "dead to sin and alive to God," trying harder to be dead to sin and alive to God, just because we know we should be, will not get us any closer to it. That is usually our default, but it will only yield the same results, not new breakthroughs.

The first step is admitting that, for many of us, we are a long way from the kind of life Paul describes. And the road forward starts with taking a step back and rethinking things completely.

Could All of This Point to Something?

Let me suggest something radical. What if our problem here is different from what we think it is?

After struggling to experience the fulfillment we know our faith promises, most of us resign ourselves to this conclusion: *It doesn't work for me.* We are not sure what the disconnect is—if something is wrong with us or if we are simply not good at living this faith thing out—but it does not seem to be working in our lives. So, we relinquish ourselves to doing the best we can, and we try not to listen to that voice that would provoke us to find something different.

But what if that is not the real problem? What if the problem is not that there is something wrong with us or that we have an inability to live this out—but that we have not seen the whole story in the first place? What if our problem is that we have been living with an incomplete Gospel?

Early Christians were first called "followers of the Way" (Acts 24:14 NIV). Our walk of faith is a journey—but like all journeys, to get to where we want to go, we need a complete set of directions. Without a complete set of directions, we will find ourselves taking wrong turns, driving in circles or running into dead ends, all the while getting more lost and frustrated.

Let's say you and I want to go see a movie. We decide what we will see and what time we will meet at the theater. Since I have never been to that theater, you give me directions to get there. But before you give them to me, you delete half of the steps—you just remove them entirely. How is my journey going to go? If I make it to the movie theater at all, I am going to be angry with you and frustrated with the situation. I would bump into you in the ticket line and express, exasperated, "These directions you gave me were terrible! I had to figure it out on my own . . ."

You may respond, "Every step in those directions was true"— and you would be correct in saying so. The steps listed *were* accurate. But they were also incomplete. And that incomplete aspect of the directions created a major problem. I needed the steps you listed, but I also needed a few more. I needed the *complete* set of directions to get where I needed to go.

What if this is what has happened with our faith? What if the Gospel we have is not wrong but incomplete? What if we do not have all of the Gospel we need in order to live it out? Until we get those missing elements, we are not going to be able to arrive at the destinations described in the promises of Scripture.

Many of us are working hard to manage elements of our faith that do not seem to be working for us. Rather than stepping back and examining the directions that guide our journey—the Gospel—many of us are focused on managing symptoms. When we spend huge amounts of energy resisting specific sin issues, we are managing symptoms. When we try harder and harder to connect with God in our times of prayer and reading Scripture, we are managing symptoms. None of this gets at the heart of the issue. But the symptoms indicate something is missing.

Let's try a different route.

This suggestion of a different route may come as a welcome relief or feel uncomfortable. On the one hand, it would allow us to be honest about where things are and how well our faith is functioning in our lives. Maybe we are not crazy. Maybe there is a reason it does not seem to be working. Maybe there is something we can do about it. Maybe we do not have to give up hope.

At the same time, what does it mean that the dearest beliefs we hold may not, in fact, be the whole story? What has been left out? What happens to our faith if we choose to let those beliefs shift?

In all likelihood, this news makes us feel both relief and discomfort. But however it feels, it is clearly an invitation into more.

The journey I describe in these pages is one I have taken. It has thrilled me, delighted me, often perplexed me and at times terrified me. It has shifted the core of my understanding of the Gospel—and therein lies the challenge. As soon as God begins to adjust our understanding of His good news, things start to get uncomfortable. I remember having some interesting conversations with God while on this journey: *God, I'm kind of concerned about these things You keep showing me in the Bible. I don't want to wind up a heretic!*

In the end, it came down to trust. Did I trust the Holy Spirit to adjust my truth, even down to my understanding of the essence of the Gospel? Could I let go of my understanding of His good news and let Him share it with me for Himself?

I thank God that He granted me the grace to walk that journey and for the life-giving understanding that came from it. Looking back, I would not trade it for anything. It has become a precious journey that God and I took together, and it is the journey I want to extend to you, as well.

I suspect you will begin to experience the same discomfort I felt. You may feel like what I present in these pages steps outside the bounds of the truth of the Gospel. You may think, as we talk, that I major on minor things and minor on major things. And that may be true—like you, I am on a journey, and I have not fully arrived. The only one who did on this earth was Jesus!

Even still, I urge you to examine the Gospel as you know it. If the Gospel is good enough that God Himself calls it the Good News, then it should probably be unbelievably, ridiculously good. Think about it. Would the best news you received in this last year have been big enough for God to call it really, really good news, let alone *the* Good News? Indeed, if the Gospel is really good news to God, it should be the kind of news that just a moment's reflection on it brings an unconscious smile to your face. It should be so good that remembering it on our worst days cheers us up. It must be so amazing that we spend the rest of our lives discovering how good it is, every day a discovery that it is even better than we realized the day before. It should be the kind of news we struggle to believe is true—in fact, the kind of news it takes faith to believe!

Most of us do not feel that way about the Gospel. Thinking of the Gospel may not cause our heart to beat a bit faster or our eyes to shine with excitement. But if the news really is the Good News, shouldn't it produce that response? We should not have to get ourselves excited about the Gospel. We should be enthralled with it!

Paul talks about not being ashamed of the Gospel:

For I am not ashamed of the gospel, for it is the power of God for salvation to everyone who believes, to the Jew first and also to the Greek.

Romans 1:16

I used to read that verse and feel a sense of burden—because if I was honest, I was kind of ashamed of the Gospel. I was not enthused about it. I read this verse as if it said, "A good Christian like Paul is excited about the Gospel, so if you're not excited, figure out a way to get there." Along with that would come feelings of shame and emotional burden.

Now I see I had that whole thing inside out. If I felt ashamed of the Gospel, then I did not have the Gospel that Paul did. This verse is not a command to get excited, but an invitation to come deeper into the truth.

What I ask of you as you read this book is twofold. First, entrust your understanding of the Gospel to God. It is His good news anyway, not yours. Give Him permission to color outside your lines if He wants to. You just might find He starts leading you into truth and setting you free.

Second, try not to let discomfort or personal history discount what we discuss. If we are talking about the heart of the Gospel, then our ideas, no matter how familiar, do not carry much weight. We should be concerned with what is in the Bible. My paradigm of the heart of the Gospel has not changed because of some experience I had—although, of course, there have been experiences along the way—but rather because God revealed things to me in His Scripture. Likewise, your point of view on the Gospel should be rooted in Scripture, not in experience. Our understanding should be in harmony with our experiences, but our theology needs to be grounded in the Word of God to be credible. That will be our concern in this book.

How Can We Get There?

For the first time, my experience of the Gospel is approaching what I described above. I find nothing more exciting to talk about, nothing more life-giving to reflect upon. The Gospel is no longer something I have to psych myself up about. It really is news so good that I struggle at times to believe God made it so good. It is incredible!

Here is a snippet of what the Good News looks like to me these days:

- The Good News is about more than just forgiveness. In fact, being saved has just as much to do with who I am as it does my heavenly report card. I am no longer looking for who I am. I am who God has made me to be, and I do not have to prove anything to anyone.
- God has eradicated everything in my being that fell at the Fall. I am no longer defined by Adam's mistakes. I am defined by Jesus' success.
- Jesus went so far as to forgive *everyone*, even those who never believe in Him. In case you are wondering, that does not mean everybody goes to heaven, but it does mean God has His arms open to welcome everyone home to Him. God is not angry with unbelievers. Instead, He watches for them to come home, like the good father of the Prodigal Son did.
- Jesus came not only to offer salvation to us, but also to kick off the story of the redemption of all creation. In fact, our salvation drafts us into the forces of light that push back the darkness in the world. We get to play the role we saw Him play during His life and ministry on the earth.

I know all that may sound crazy. It seems like some of those statements could not possibly be true. They are audacious—absurd! How could we believe those things about ourselves? It would be prideful to believe them, right?

These are the very questions I asked in my journey through this, and I do think it is important to ask them. However, if these statements are the truth revealed in God's Scripture, then we have a responsibility to embrace them. After all, the Gospel belongs to Him, not us.

As we work through the questions that arise on this journey and we begin to see how all of this is rooted in Scripture, an amazing thing happens: Other parts of us come alive, and our heart fills with hope. Rather than feeling like a distant figure, God becomes alive and active. Our life begins to orbit around a new story: *I am who He made me to be.*

I cannot see myself now without seeing the work of God. As a result, my life and my journey are stitched irrevocably to Him. My faith has come alive in a way it never did before. One of my closest friends put it this way when he heard this truth for the first time: "It's like being born again, again."

Our hearts come alive as they resonate with the truth God has already written on them. Sin tendencies fall away. Jesus becomes a bigger and bigger part of our everyday reality and experience. Our struggle with God feeling distant vanishes, and our effectiveness for the Gospel skyrockets.

What if the Gospel is as good as God promises it is? Wouldn't you want to discover that and live in light of it? What if you could live above sin because Jesus really defeated it? What if you could walk in close communion with God and be empowered to represent Him well? What if the exhortations to "count our trials as joy" became the sensible thing to do instead of feeling like an impossible standard? What if we could love ourselves without feeling like a disappointment?

I am increasingly convinced this is what a life with God looks like. Again, I love the way my friend expressed his experience of discovering the Gospel afresh: "It's like being born again, again." This has been the journey for me, as well. I have stepped into a whole new layer of belief and experience of my faith, and I have been freed in ways I did not know were possible. It may be hard to believe there is that much more available to you in your faith, but there is—and our journey through the rest of these pages will lead you there.

THINKING LIKE JESUS

- For many of us, the faith we experience often falls far short of what we see promised to us in Scripture.
- Rather than working harder at a faith that is not working, our understanding of the Gospel needs to be reworked.

2

The Gospel I Thought I Knew

Sometimes the most amazing journeys begin not in our dramatic moments but in our mundane ones. The journey I describe in these pages began, for me, while I sat at our dining room table with my younger brother, Daniel, and our good friend Andrew. We were talking about what God had been doing in our lives and what we saw on the horizon. This was not an uncommon event. We had known each other twenty years, and God had wrapped our spiritual journeys together in an intricate weave of His sovereignty.

I tapped my fingers on the table and reflected out loud as something came to my awareness for the first time. I said, "If I'm honest, I don't really understand what happened on the cross. I mean, what happened to the Law? I think I know the 'right' answer, but it doesn't seem like it really adds up . . . I guess that's something I should figure out . . ."

I grew up in the church. From about the second week of my life, church has been a fixture in my experience of life.

The church I called home was an amazing fellowship of about four hundred people in the Chicagoland area that loved Jesus and each other. In that church, I learned the value of Scripture and of understanding theology. I developed a passion for seeing God change people's lives, and I learned how to walk with Jesus in the rhythms of study and prayer. I count myself fortunate to have been rooted in the things of the faith so young in my life.

The pastor of my home church was saved while reading the book of Romans and devoted a sermon series to that book every year. Pastor Dave, as everybody called him, loved theology and teaching. As such, growing up in that church, I received a good dose of both.

By the time I got to college, Pastor Dave had taught me much of what was covered in my Christian Theology course. Several years later, through my graduate studies, my thinking only continued to be refined and my understanding only continued to grow as I explored various theological points of view.

All of this being the case, I was not asking for an explanation of what happened at the cross when I voiced what I did at the table that day. I could have told you what was written in the systematic theology books. Rather, I was seeing that the Gospel as I understood it did not fit together as tightly as had been conveyed to me. It did not seem logically self-coherent. I was "dead to sin" (Romans 6:11), but I was still a sinner. Jesus was "the Lamb of God, who takes away the sins of the world" (John 1:29), but only Christians were forgiven; everyone else was under God's wrath.

My scientific training might have helped me see the problems here. At the time, I was working toward my Ph.D. in theoretical quantum physics at the University of Illinois, and I was learning how scientific models work. A scientific model offers a descriptive explanation for what happens in a particular situation, based on what the data reveals. The more the data correlates with the description, the stronger the model is believed to be. Any outliers, or exceptions, to the data become opportunities for new study and discovery. At the top of the twentieth century, this kind of inquiry is what led to the discovery of the relativity theory and quantum mechanics.

You could say our explanation of the Gospel is similar. While I would not call our explanation of the Gospel a scientific model—calling it a mental model would be more accurate—it develops in much the same way a scientific model does. It makes sense of the "data" we find in Scripture. It gets stronger the more it correlates with the data points of Scripture. And just like what happens in scientific study, when we find exceptions in the data (Scripture) that seem to contradict the model we have developed (Gospel), we are faced with an opportunity to study more and ask questions. We are given a chance to ask, What is really going on here?

After that evening I began to search Scripture and ask God to show me what I did not see. I read the book of Romans, especially chapters 6–8, over and over again. I pored over them in prayer and study. I read the rest of Paul's letters, then went back to Romans again. Over and over, for months, I asked God to reveal to me the Gospel as He understood it.

During this process, it felt like my understanding was increasingly breaking down. I began to see more and more holes in how I understood the Gospel. What was "the flesh," and how was it connected to sin? What did it mean to be saved? What did it mean to be a sinner? For a season, all of these questions felt like they were shifting sand beneath my feet.

Eventually, a new understanding emerged—but only after God shook my previous understanding enough so that my hands dropped what He wanted me to drop and I could receive what He wanted me to receive.

One thing I learned is this: We cannot take a journey by staying in the same spot. To travel the road, we must leave our homes; we do not get the option of taking both.

Home is comfortable. It is warm and inviting, but the road out there seems long and uncertain. It winds into the distant fog, and we wonder if we will lose our bearings while we are on it. I find that I usually stay where I am until it becomes uncomfortable or loses its appeal. I want to stay in the same place, but something prods me out the door. For most of us, it is only when the familiarity of staying home is more painful than the change of hitting the road that we undertake the journey.

This chapter is going to poke holes in what may be your "home" Gospel. It is not meant to demean anyone who holds these beliefs—after all, they are the same beliefs I held for most of my life—but rather to pose important questions and create the discomfort we need to begin this new journey.

Poking Holes in the Gospel

Let me outline the Gospel as I knew it. It is one that, as I have shared it with various audiences, I have found is a common baseline understanding of the core of the Gospel:

- Man was created to be in relationship with God, but man sinned, and sin cuts us off from relationship with God.
- The only way to pay the price for that sin is to die, but death outside of relationship with God sends you to hell for eternity.
- Jesus came and offered His life to pay for our sins, which He did by dying on the cross.

- When we place our faith in Jesus, His payment for sin on the cross is applied to us. We are forgiven and put back into relationship with God. Because of our restored relationship with God, we go to heaven when we die.

This was the Gospel as I understood it from my evangelical upbringing. While there may be additional nuances included in different groups—if you are charismatic, for example, there may be elements about the Holy Spirit or the Kingdom of God thrown in—this is generally understood to be the core of the Gospel.

As we discussed in the last chapter, something about the core Gospel message is not complete. What will complete the set of directions, so to speak? What will give us the full picture? We must look for what is missing.

To do so, I am going to ask a few critical questions about the picture of the Gospel drawn above. We will not wind up anywhere questionable, like saying Jesus did not forgive our sins or that everyone is saved, whether they believe in Jesus or not. But we need to assess our current understanding to determine what is working and what is not.

So, let's begin.

Hole #1: What does it mean that sin cuts us off from relationship with God?

The outline of the Gospel above starts with the idea that sin separates us from God and breaks our relationship with Him. In fact, this is often taken to be the essential definition of *sin*: whatever cuts off our relationship with God. The problem is that this idea does not coincide with the way we see Jesus acted during His ministry on earth.

Let's begin by remembering that Jesus is the central revelation of who God is and what He is really like:

Jesus said to him, "Have I been with you so long, and you still do not know me, Philip? Whoever has seen me has seen the Father. How can you say, 'Show us the Father'?"

John 14:9

Long ago, at many times and in many ways, God spoke to our fathers by the prophets, but in these last days he has spoken to us by his Son. . . . He is the radiance of the glory of God and the exact imprint of his nature.

Hebrews 1:1–3

Jesus is the exact picture of God. He alone fully and completely reveals what God is like.

And yet when Jesus was on the earth, people's sin did not cut them off from relationship with Him. In fact, Jesus surrounded Himself with people who were loaded with sin: prostitutes, cheating tax collectors and other people like that. Time and time again, He related to people, even in the moment of their sin, and it was relationship with Him that provided the road forward for them to step out of their sin.

Consider the woman caught in adultery and brought to Jesus, or when Jesus ate with Zacchaeus. Jesus opened a relationship with them while they were still in their sin, and He empowered them to get out of it. Who was it He could not tolerate? The religious leaders who were trying to be perfect.

We might think Jesus overlooked the sins of unbelievers in an effort to evangelize them, but even in His relationships with His disciples, who were already evangelizing others, sin did not introduce a divide that made relationship impossible. Consider Peter's denial of Jesus and his subsequent restoration after the resurrection. Peter was the one who ran away from relationship with Jesus by picking up his old life and going back to fishing (see John 21:2–3). Jesus came after him and reconciled the relationship (see verses 4–22), which means God desired and pursued a relationship with Peter, even after Peter sinned. Peter's sin made Peter pull away from Jesus, but Jesus did not pull away from Peter.

Now, please do not hear what I am not saying. I am not saying sin does not cause problems or that Jesus did not need to come handle those problems. Sin certainly introduces problems, and Jesus definitely brought the answer to them!

I am not even saying Adam and Eve were not cut off from relationship with God because of sin. I am simply observing that this idea—that sin cuts us off from relationship with God—is not in line with how Jesus operated when He interacted with sinners. If our faith is supposed to revolve around Jesus, that seems like a legitimate issue to me. Perhaps, then, our understanding of sin is too simple and cannot be captured solely by the idea of separation from God.

It is easy to dismiss a different perspective about how sin affects our relationship with God because it is not how we are used to processing the meaning of Scripture. I understand that, and I do think we need a compelling reason to ever reconsider a central tenet of our faith. That being said, any frame of theology that does not match what is clearly written in Scripture must be rethought, too. If Jesus hung out with sinners—and did so almost recreationally—then a cornerstone of our salvation understanding needs to be compatible with that fact.

Hole #2: How much does the resurrection matter?

Another important issue with the classic understanding of the Gospel is that the resurrection of Jesus is treated as an afterthought. In fact, I did not even mention the resurrection in the description earlier. Did you notice that? If not, this is because the resurrection does not flow in the theological line of thought we carry of the Gospel. It is an added bonus: Of course, we do not want Jesus to stay dead. But from a salvation point of view, it is not treated as a critical part of the story.

Jesus is the sin sacrifice for us, our understanding of the Gospel tells us. Once that sacrifice has been made, we are forgiven. We know this because of the Old Testament, where sin sacrifices were made frequently for the forgiveness of sins. But those animals were never raised to new life. Why, then, did Jesus resurrect? Does the resurrection carry theological importance? Somehow our Gospel got fixed on Jesus' death and has largely overlooked His resurrection.

The resurrection does carry great theological importance, but to see that importance clearly, we have to see which parts of the Gospel are omitted from the description above—like the parts of the driving directions I did not have when I made that trip to the theater in chapter 1.

You can see the imbalance of this theological emphasis of the crucifixion over the resurrection in the testimony of Church history. Perhaps this is a little simplistic, but which holiday do we celebrate more: Good Friday or Easter? The answer is Easter, of course. Why is it, then, that Church tradition focuses on the resurrection, but our Gospel focuses on the crucifixion?

Furthermore, in Scripture, Paul ties salvation not just to the death of Jesus but also to His resurrection. It was not enough to believe Jesus died for your sins, according to Paul. Believing Jesus was resurrected was also critically important to salvation:

> If you confess with your mouth that Jesus is Lord and believe in your heart *that God raised him from the dead*, you will be saved.
>
> Romans 10:9, emphasis mine

According to Paul, I cannot be saved if I only believe Jesus' death was a sin sacrifice for me. Receiving His resurrection by faith is critical to my salvation, as well. In fact, notice what Paul does *not* say: that you must believe Jesus paid for your sins. Paul says you simply have to believe Jesus died and was resurrected, whether or not you think that has anything to do with your sins.

Indeed, the whole notion we usually carry of how Jesus dealt with sin does not seem to square with what Paul believed. If it did, he would not have written some of the things he did, like this:

> And if Christ has not been raised, your faith is futile and you are still in your sins.
>
> 1 Corinthians 15:17

Take a moment and think about that. Paul is saying that if Jesus had died but not been resurrected, our sins would not have been taken care of. In whatever way Paul understood the crucifixion and resurrection of Jesus, it was not the way we usually understand it—that Jesus' death on the cross took care of our sins. Paul said the resurrection was a necessary part of it.

Again, like what happened with animals in the Old Testament, Jesus' being a sin sacrifice on our behalf would not have required the resurrection, just the cross. The reality of our no longer being "still in our sins" must include more than forgiveness.

Now, in case you are getting nervous, let me reassure you: I do believe Jesus was the sin sacrifice for us. That is certainly an aspect of the Gospel. He did provide forgiveness for our sins, and we all need to be eternally grateful for that.

The question at hand, however, is whether this is the *entirety* of the Gospel. I do not believe it is. In addition, making it the entirety of the Gospel may cause us to miss a major thrust of the New Testament.

Hole #3: Do Jesus and Paul speak different messages?

As Christians, we believe there is only one Gospel. Paul makes this clear:

> I am astonished that you are so quickly deserting him who called you in the grace of Christ and are turning to a different gospel—*not that there is another one*, but there are some who trouble you and want to distort the gospel of Christ.
>
> Galatians 1:6–7, emphasis mine

But it can be quite confusing to pin down what that one Gospel is. Honestly, it can even be difficult to pin down what it should be called!

Here is what I mean. In the first five books of the New Testament—Matthew, Mark, Luke, John and Acts—the main focus is the Kingdom of God (or the Kingdom of heaven, as Matthew puts it). Jesus preaches and teaches about the Kingdom everywhere He goes (see Matthew 9:35; Mark 1:14–15). The disciples and the Pharisees ask about the Kingdom (see Matthew 18:1; Luke 17:20). Jesus sends His disciples out to preach the Kingdom of God (see Matthew 10:7; Luke 10:9). If you determined the Gospel based solely on the four gospels and the book of Acts, you would probably say the Gospel is called the Gospel of the Kingdom of God.

Once you flip the page to Romans, however, Paul does not seem nearly as invested in the message of the Kingdom of God. Sure, sometimes he talks about it (see Romans 14:17; 1 Corinthians 4:20), but mostly he focuses on another message that he also calls the Gospel: *the Gospel of righteousness by faith* (see Romans 1:16–17; 3:22). He talks about salvation by grace through faith (see Ephesians 2:8) and the issue of personal sin (see Romans 3:23). Much of the writing revolves around these two terms:

righteousness and *grace*. If you were to read only Paul's letters, you would probably come to the conclusion that the Gospel is the message of salvation by grace through faith in Jesus Christ.

In case you have not previously noticed this sharp contrast, I counted the number of occurrences of these words in the two locations:

	Verses with Kingdom	Verses with *Righteousness* or *Grace*
Gospels and Acts	128	40
Paul's Letters	14	149

These two portions of the New Testament have a different focus—and they both call their major portion of discussion "the Gospel." Which Gospel is it? Or do we have multiple Gospels? What is happening?

We cannot simply argue they are the same Gospel with different terms, either. At the very least, this suggestion breaks down because the context between the two is different. The message of the Kingdom of God is a *cosmic* message. It tells of the restoration of God's Kingdom through the timeline of human history. It has to do with the overthrowing of Satan's dominion and the presence of God's will on earth. We find this to be the case in a few key passages:

"Your kingdom come, your will be done, on earth as it is in heaven."

Matthew 6:10

"Now is the judgment of this world; now will the ruler of this world be cast out. And I, when I am lifted up from the earth, will draw all people to myself."

John 12:31–32

The message of righteousness by faith, on the other hand, is a *personal* message. It discusses our personal sin and our own renewal before God. It is a story of individual restoration, not the restoration of all things. Paul makes this clear here:

> For one will scarcely die for a righteous person—though perhaps for a good person one would even dare to die—but God shows his love for us in that while we were still sinners, Christ died for us.
>
> Romans 5:7–8

> For by grace you have been saved through faith. And this is not your own doing; it is the gift of God, not a result of works, so that no one may boast.
>
> Ephesians 2:8–9

This conundrum has been well known for a long time and still causes a lot of head-scratching to this day, even among top Christian scholars. I read an article a few years ago in *Christianity Today* titled "Jesus vs. Paul"—the title alone captures it all.[1] How do we reconcile our two Gospels? What actually is our message?

This is a big deal, and we cannot afford a lack of clarity here. In my experience, many believers identify with one of these two messages and capitalize on that message while not giving the other much attention. Charismatics often focus on the message of the Kingdom, and those identifying as evangelical adhere more closely to the message of righteousness by faith in Christ. If you find yourself thinking, *But this one is the real Gospel*, you are choosing one over the other. If we think in either/or terms, we do not understand everything happening in Scripture.

Perhaps this is not a concern for you. It was not for me until I started attending a charismatic church after having grown up as an evangelical. It took me a long time to pin down what my new church believed because its term *Gospel* meant something different from what I was used to. Eventually, I realized these different camps of the Church had radically different messages. Both had scriptural support for calling their Good News the Gospel.

Have you ever experienced the tension of realizing a large portion of the Church has a conviction about the core of the Gospel that differs from yours—and that they have Scripture to back it up? Even if you have not experienced this situation yourself, it should raise some concern. Shouldn't the Church, as a whole, agree on the Gospel?

Hole #4: Why did Jesus have to die?

The final question I would like to consider is this: What is it that required Jesus to offer His life? Why did the Son of God have to come and die?

The understanding of the Gospel that paints Jesus as a sin sacrifice offers no clear answer to this question. The reality is that before Jesus came and died, there was already a way to obtain forgiveness of sins: the sacrificial system of the Old Testament. By going to the priest to offer the proper animal and following the appropriate sin-sacrifice ritual, you could have your sins forgiven and be put back in good standing with God. It was a functional system that worked. The author of Hebrews tells us:

> Indeed, under the law almost everything is purified with blood, and without the shedding of blood there is no forgiveness of sins.
>
> Hebrews 9:22

It was not that the forgiveness of sins "sort of" worked under the Old Covenant. It *did* work. Those sins were forgiven. Those who were not Jewish could leave their native lands and ways and become foreigners who followed God (see Isaiah 56:6–7). So, before Jesus ever set foot on the earth, a solution to the forgiveness issue for every people group already existed.

With all that in place, why did Jesus have to die? If the mechanism for forgiving sins required only the blood of animals, should not we expect the blood of the Son of God to be more effective somehow—to do something more? Of course, Jesus only died once, whereas animal sacrifices were offered repeatedly, but that is exactly the point. Should not Jesus' blood do more for us than the blood from a bunch of animals does? Should it not be more effective than that?

If the blood of Jesus is qualitatively more effective than the blood of animals, what would that mean? It would mean that Jesus' death and resurrection did give us everything that was possible under the sacrificial system, meaning forgiveness of sins. But it also gives us more. It would mean there is more to the Gospel story than the picture painted at the beginning of this chapter.

If that is the case, what are we missing? And how much does what we are missing affect our lives?

Discovering the Gospel Anew

You may feel uncomfortable considering these questions. I understand that. And I will say again that I do believe Jesus' death paid the price for our sins and that because of His death our sins are forgiven and that a relational barrier between ourselves and God has been removed. Absolutely, I believe these things. It is just that now I believe these things *and more*.

In my own journey with these questions, I began to piece together that I had defined my understanding of the Gospel by what I was saved *from* rather than what I was saved *to*. In this book, I want to introduce you to this second idea. Why? Because the Gospel must be more than the completion of the Old Covenant.

The story many of us believe about the Gospel begins to break down because it completes the Old Covenant but gives us no understanding of the New Covenant. We have come to understand everything through the lens of the Law and the sacrifices of the Jews—sin debt, the sacrifice to forgive sins, the restoration of our standing with God and so forth. All of that is true, but it comes solely out of the Old Covenant. It describes what you were saved from and what no longer applies to you. Now that all those things are taken care of in Jesus, what *does* apply to you? What are you saved *to*? Where are you headed?

Think about it this way. When I leave work every day, I get in my car, start the engine and drive in the direction of my home. I do this every day without thinking, as most of us do. To get to where we want to go, we move toward our destination. I could try something different. I could try walking out the door, getting in my car, facing the church I just left and then driving in reverse the whole way home. I think we all know what would happen if I did that. Even if I could navigate the turns and stoplights, I would not be able to see the traffic and would inevitably get in an accident.

You cannot take a journey by focusing on where you were. You have to take a journey by focusing on where you are headed. When we define our Gospel through the lens of the Old Covenant, we are driving in reverse, focused on where we used to be rather than where we are going. We define our faith by the completion of what no longer applies to us, rather than looking ahead to what applies to us now.

If this describes your belief system—if you are more focused on what you are saved from than what you are saved to—then

I invite you to expand your understanding of the Gospel by discovering where we are headed. Now that Jesus has completed the Old Covenant for us, what is the New Covenant? What applies to us now, and how do we live in light of it?

This is exactly what we are going to explore in the rest of this book. Our starting point for that journey looks at how the Gospel fits into the cosmic story of human history.

THINKING LIKE JESUS

- The Gospel, as defined by the story of Jesus being the sin sacrifice for humanity, is part of the Gospel story but not the whole of it.
- The prevailing story of the Gospel identifies Jesus as the completion of the Old Covenant but does not give us a solid grasp on the New Covenant Jesus ushered in. This is one reason we feel stranded and struggle to live the Christian life after we are saved.

3

Reframing
the Question

Einstein.
The name evokes a brilliant, eccentric and playful scientist who almost single-handedly turned on its head humanity's understanding of how God stitched the world together. Even now, more than a hundred years after he published his famous equations describing relativity, Einstein's reputation endures as the standard for intelligence and unusual perception. His name has become synonymous with *genius*.

Einstein is best known for his theory of relativity. This theory revealed that space, time, matter and gravity are not what they appear to be. Rather than the unchanging entities we assume they are, the theory of relativity depicts them as intertwined, flexible quantities that twist and turn into each other in different situations.

With the publication of his theories of special relativity and general relativity in the early twentieth century, Einstein revolutionized the scientific community's understanding of matter, space, time and energy. The application of his theories led to the development of nuclear power, lasers, GPS, digital cameras and more. We have Einstein to thank for much of our lifestyle in this information age.

In the ten years that followed the publication of Einstein's theory of general relativity, the scientific community built on his ideas and began to explore a new arena of science: quantum mechanics. It was as if the world was being rebirthed, and a new and fantastic picture of the world of atoms emerged. Quantum mechanics explains how the building blocks of the universe behave, and it turns out that reality is stranger than fiction here. The scientists who developed quantum mechanics quipped, "If you feel quantum mechanics makes sense, you have not properly understood the theory."

Einstein was involved in the development of this budding understanding, yet this pillar of the scientific community was not as central to that process as you might expect. In fact, as the field developed, he began to resist some of the conclusions at which the scientific community was arriving. Quantum mechanics was built on a different premise than relativity, one where the sense of causality—the idea that one event triggers another—begins to break down and is traded for a world that bounces around on a sea of unpredictable quantum fluctuations. Randomness is encoded at the core of quantum mechanics, and this was an idea Einstein simply could not get on board with. This tension resulted in one of his most famous statements: "As I have said so many times, God doesn't play dice with the world."

For the record, Einstein was not professing faith here. He did not believe in a personal God, and it seems he never landed at much of a belief, other than understanding there must have been some higher force that caused the order we see in the physical world. Rather, Einstein was expressing a profound distaste for some of the central ideas upon which the theory of quantum mechanics hangs.

As the tale of history tells, Einstein began to change directions. He attempted to develop a "unifying theory" that would encapsulate and explain both relativity and quantum mechanics, while removing the unsavory parts of the latter. In undertaking this effort, Einstein distanced himself even more from the mainstream scientific community. While quantum mechanics was gaining tremendous traction through experimental verification and its predictive power, Einstein's work became theoretical to the point of detaching from reality—the *coup de grâce* for a scientist's career. He was unable to accept the world as it was and instead tried to invent the world he wanted in his mind. He never succeeded in his quest and gradually drifted into irrelevance in the scientific community before his death. At the time he passed away, he was respected as a legendary mind, albeit a peripheral one. The ultimate "rock star" of scientific invention was "relatively" left behind before his career was over.

Where did Einstein go wrong? Einstein did not like the core assumptions of quantum mechanics, so he continued along the path that made him comfortable.

Many of us are prone to the same behavior. When confronted with a problem where we do not seem to be making noticeable progress, we assume we must, at least, be heading in the right direction. We believe if we continue along the same path, we will eventually get there; we just have not given it enough effort yet.

This is what makes a person refuse to stop and ask for directions, even though he is hopelessly lost; he assumes he needs to keep going a little farther and he will figure it out. It is also what keeps us in jobs that fit us poorly; even though we may not be good at what we do or may find it unsatisfying, we keep going, hoping the situation will change. And it is what keeps us in relationships that subtract from our lives instead of add to them; we want to believe a turbulent relationship is just about to settle down and become a healthier one. We keep hoping we are "right around the corner" from this change; we just can't see it yet.

In my experience, trying the same thing, only harder, usually does not lead to drastic progress. Usually, the problem is that I am considering the situation from the wrong point of view. What is needed is not more effort but a different perspective.

For example, suppose someone is stuck in a job that is a poor fit for them. They are not very good at the job, and they do not find it rewarding. They have two ways of viewing the situation. First, they can view the situation through the lens of what they will have to give up if they leave, such as financial security, valued relationships or social status. In this case, they will likely try to make the situation work, possibly even for years, hoping that something will change. They will work hard to make the most of a bad situation.

But what if that person sees the situation not for what they have to give up if they leave but for what they are already giving up by staying? Every week, they give forty-plus hours to something that does not contribute to their sense of significance or tap in to the talents God has given them. Every week, the best of what God has put in them is wasted. This person will probably make the most of the situation for a while and then find a new situation.

Now let's apply this to what we are after in this book. We have already seen that our traditional approach to the Gospel does not always work the way the Bible says it should. We are meant to live abundant lives, but we do not live them. We are meant to be free from sin's entanglements, but we are all knotted up inside our bad habits and compulsions. Trying harder has not brought us very far.

Similarly, in the last chapter, we looked at several questions that point out significant problems in our Gospel's premise. We began to notice holes, and it can be troubling to know which direction to head next.

So, what do we do? Do we go after those problem questions directly?

I suggest we try on a different lens. Rather than beat our fists against the problems we now see, I am going to take us through a process of reexamining our approach. When our answers stop working, it is time to change our questions.

I love questions because they can lead us to new perspectives. So much of what I have learned in faith has come because I have simply asked our Teacher, Jesus, questions. I would encourage you to do the same.

So, let's start by changing the question. Rather than asking, "What is the sin problem?" or "How do Jesus and Paul fit together?" let's ask, "If the Gospel is good news, what is the bad news?" In other words, if the Gospel is God's cosmic answer, what problem did He solve?

To see what God put right, let's look at what went wrong. And to look at that, we need to return to the beginning.

A Beginning Word

Genesis 1–3 tells the story of the opening of the human drama. The first chapter begins with an explosive symphony of God's creation process. He speaks light into the darkness and proceeds to create the skies, waters, plants and so forth by speaking them forth. Building block by building block, God declares creation into being, until we arrive at the pinnacle of the process: the creation of man.

At this point, God does something interesting. He changes up the pattern. He *does* speak, but in a different way. Rather than speak Adam into being, He speaks something into being *over* humanity:

> Then God said, "Let us make man in our image, after our likeness. And let them have dominion over the fish of the sea and over the birds of the heavens and over the livestock and over all the earth and over every creeping thing that creeps on the earth."
>
> Genesis 1:26

God declares His image and likeness over Adam and then assigns him a dominion. Then He sculpts Adam and fills him with His Spirit:

> The LORD God formed the man of dust from the ground and breathed into his nostrils the breath of life, and the man became a living creature.
>
> Genesis 2:7

This is so interesting to me. God broke the pattern of creation for humanity. I believe He did this because He wanted to draw our attention to what He actually created in this moment. It was not Adam or Eve. It was something altogether different. God spoke and created an *identity* and a *destiny* for humanity.

First, an Identity

The first thing God spoke into being over humanity was a stated identity. He spoke who we fundamentally are. And what was that? God said we were made "in [God's] image, after [His] likeness." This is the true essence of humanity, as declared by our Creator. We are images of God.

What does it mean to be God's image? That is a great question, and I suggest you consult your wallet. No, I am not trying to solicit your money, but pull out any bills you have in there and look at the front of them. You may recognize such faces as George Washington, Abraham Lincoln or other notable former presidents.

Now, let's suppose you have a one-dollar bill. Take a few seconds to look at George's face on that bill. Is that the real George Washington on that bill? No, of course not. It is the *image* of George Washington. In reality, that image is just ink on paper. Yet if George Washington were to miraculously walk into the room right now, I guarantee you would recognize him. Why? Because you have been surrounded by his image. You have never seen the real George Washington, but his image has created your ability to recognize him.

It is the same for us. We were created in God's image. That means we were created to be "a recognition" of God. The rest of creation was to look at humanity and see not the dust we were made of but who God is through us. *Wow, that's what He's really like?* That was meant to be the response of the animals and even the heavenly realms when they beheld humanity.

I can imagine this idea is hard to swallow. We have become conditioned to see ourselves as anything but what God has said we are. We think dim thoughts about ourselves and overlook who God is and who He created us to be. We allow so much junk to define us that has nothing to do with God's definition of us at all.

We need to steer clear of this poor view of ourselves, even if we think it is true.

I like to think of it this way. My wife is a musician. She teaches voice and piano to a variety of students, and she has a lovely soprano voice. Sometimes she will sing in other languages—French, Italian or German. And even though I do not understand the words when she sings in those foreign languages, I still enjoy it.

But because I do not know the language, at times I can misunderstand the purpose of a piece as I listen to it. Without the words to guide me, I can mistake the heart of it. Perhaps I think a song of despair is really a song about quiet hope. Maybe a song that sounds vengeful to me is actually a song about the fear of a foreboding war.

When I do not understand the purpose of the song, I do what we all do: I consult the words the artist penned. Why? Because the artist is the one who determines what the song is about. I can think whatever I want about the song, but the artist is the one who created it, and the artist gets to determine its meaning. If I disagree, the conclusion is rather straightforward: I am wrong!

In the same way, if we do not see the original purpose of humanity to be what our Creator said it is—to be the image of God on the earth—then we are wrong. God is inviting us to see ourselves through His eyes.

Second, a Destiny

Along with speaking into being our identity, God spoke into being our destiny. And this makes sense. If we are made in the image of the King of kings, we need to exercise some sort of rule. To that end, God gave humanity rule, or dominion, over everything that came forth from the earth.

Adam immediately set about the business of ruling in God's image by naming the animals:

> Now out of the ground the LORD God had formed every beast of the field and every bird of the heavens and brought them to the man to see what he would call them. And whatever the man called every living creature, that was its name.
>
> Genesis 2:19

I think, in our Western perspective, we can miss what is happening here. Remember that to an Eastern mindset, which was the audience to whom Genesis was written, a name was not just a label that identified someone. It was a person's nature revealed.

You can see this at play in the way the Hebrews named their children. They gave names that reflected the essence of their child's nature.

We do not have that same practice. In English, we adopt names from other languages. We might name our children Jonathan, Olivia or Aiden, which are Hebrew, Greek and Irish in origin, respectively. But we lose touch with the idea that these names actually mean something in the original language when they are bestowed on someone. It would be similar to naming a child "Laughter" or "Victorious." Each time we spoke their name, we would be speaking the meaning of who they are. This is why it was significant whenever God renamed someone in Scripture. It was an anchor point for the essence of the person.

So, when Adam named the animals, he was not calling them any old name. He was assigning them a nature. That's why it says, "Whatever the man called every living creature, that was its *name*" (emphasis mine).

Imagine it: God forms an animal and brings it to Adam. While standing there, Adam looks it over and says, "This one will be called Dog." *Bang*—the animal begins panting and nuzzling Adam's leg.

God brings another animal to Adam and waits. "Hmmm," Adam says. "I think I'll call this one Cat!" *Poof*—the cat meows and walks away, never to be seen in the Garden again.

I think it really was like that. (Well, maybe not *exactly* like that.)

What was Adam doing? The same thing God did in Genesis 1. Rather than "Let there be light," Adam was saying, "Let there be Dog." The principle and process were the same. Each one spoke, and something was. God created from nothing, and Adam spoke—and ruled over—what was brought forth from the earth.

A Tumble Downward

As you know, the story does not stop there. The tragic event of the Fall happens. Satan deceives Eve, and Adam and Eve eat the fruit of the Tree of Knowledge of Good and Evil. Sin enters the story, as does our need for a Savior. Let's consider what this means for our intended identity and dominion.

First, concerning identity, I find the interchange between the serpent and Eve very interesting. This is what Satan offers Eve for disobeying God and eating the fruit she has been told not to eat:

> "For God knows that when you eat of it your eyes will be opened, *and you will be like God*, knowing good and evil."
>
> Genesis 3:5, emphasis mine

How does Satan tempt Eve? By telling her she will be like God. But she is already like God! That was how she was created, remember? She was not created to be anything other than like God, and yet, somehow, she forgets that in the moment.

Maybe she had a bad hair day. Maybe the serpent was a really good liar. Whatever the case, something terribly tragic happens here. Satan offers her a lie—that she was not like God—and a solution: "If you eat my fruit, you will be like Him. Looks good, right?"

Here is the bitter irony: When Eve believed and acted on Satan's lie, his lie became her truth. She was like God, until she ate the fruit.

In fact, the likeness of God was traded in a profound way. I believe it was no coincidence that Adam and Eve committed a sin that moved from their outsides to their insides. As they ate the fruit of the Tree of Knowledge of Good and Evil, that fruit metabolized and became part of their physical bodies. The sin they committed became part of their being. They were fractured at their very core.

Human beings always manifest what is happening inside of them. This is why, for example, it is not fun to be around someone who has a bad attitude. They draw from the negativity within and put it into the environment around them. A positive person, on the other hand, draws us into their positivity. This inborn ability was given so we could display the God who desires to dwell within us. But with sin now resident within humanity, the image Adam and Eve displayed was no longer the image of God. It was the image of sin.

As Paul discussed in Romans 7, the issue is far more than skin deep. It goes to the core. The sin problem of humanity is not just sinful actions that need forgiveness. It is also the sin image that we now bear instead of the image of God. Paul went so far as to say sin had the ability to act within him. It was a dynamic and active force within his person that manifested through his actions:

> Now if I do what I do not want, it is no longer I who do it, but sin that dwells within me.
>
> Romans 7:20

Here is what we need to understand: The image of God in us has been hijacked by the image of sin. Furthermore, sin works its ugly way from the inside to the outside of us. After Adam and Eve took sin inside themselves, it was not long before they shifted the blame of their mistakes to each other and hid from God.

This is a big point and one worth dwelling on a bit more. I just told you the root of our sin concern is not sins that have been committed but sin that dwells within us. In other words, it is not behavioral; it is ontological. It relates to our being. Who we are at the core is fractured by sin. In fact, that shattered being is the root that causes our sinful behavior.

It is like this. Picture you have a dandelion in your yard. It is fully grown and showing its yellow head in your otherwise-pristine yard of smooth green grass. Of course, you want to remove the invader, so you walk over to the offender, bend down and pull the flower and all its leaves out of the ground. Have you solved the problem? Only temporarily. In a week, it will be back, and you will have to repeat the process. In fact, you can attack the surface of that plant all summer, if you choose, but it will keep resurfacing until you get underneath the ground and pull the plant out by the roots.

In the same way, humanity has sinful actions; these are like the leaves and flower of the dandelion. These sinful actions are real and need to be dealt with—but they flow from something deeper: sin's residence in the very fibers of our being. We could address the sinful actions all day long and never get to the root of the issue.

This is, in fact, what happened in the Old Testament. As we have already seen, the system in place to deal with sinful actions involved going to the Temple, interfacing with a priest and performing animal sacrifices. Recall the verse we saw in the last chapter:

> Indeed, under the law almost everything is purified with blood, and without the shedding of blood there is no forgiveness of sins.
>
> Hebrews 9:22

Under the Law, blood was required to *forgive* sins. Blood dealt with sinful actions. Yet notice what the author goes on to say a few verses later:

> For since the law has but a shadow of the good things to come instead of the true form of these realities, it can never, by the same sacrifices that are continually offered every year, make perfect those who draw near. . . . But in these sacrifices there is a reminder of sins every year. For it is impossible for the blood of bulls and goats to take away sins.
>
> Hebrews 10:1, 3–4

Those blood sacrifices forgave sins, but they could not address the deeper issue. It was like pulling the head and leaves of the dandelion out of the ground but leaving the root in the soil. Blood sacrifices could not make the people perfect or remove their inherent sin. In fact, they functioned as a reminder of that sin instead. Because the Jews had to keep going back to the Temple each year, they could not escape the truth that they were powerless to stop sinning. Sin within them produced its ugly fruit, and there was no sufficient means to address it.

In fact, I would suggest that the term *sinner* in Scripture has more to do with the people that sin lives within than it does the people who have committed sinful actions. Paul writes about how people became sinners:

> For as by the one man's disobedience the many were made sinners.
>
> Romans 5:19

Are we made guilty by association with Adam's failures? Did his bad record get passed on to us? No. Instead, his broken template was passed along to us. Once Adam and Eve sinned and became sinners—people in whom sin dwells—they reproduced that broken template throughout the human race. They could not pass along anything other than what they were, and that was the image of God, fractured and broken by sin.

Here is how I think of it. Inside an apple are seeds. Those seeds contain everything that is needed to grow another apple tree, given the right conditions. You might say there is an apple tree inside each apple. In fact, inside every apple is an apple tree that will bear more apples and, hence, more trees. So, inside every apple is a *forest* that could cover a large area, given the right growth conditions.

Now, whatever happens to that apple affects the whole forest that comes after it. If I eat the apple and throw the seeds away, that whole forest is erased. If I genetically modified the DNA in the seeds, changing the color of the leaves from green to blue, the whole forest would shift, as well, producing an orchard of blue-leaved apples. This is because the original apple is the template. It is the pattern for all the others after it. Its nature gets passed down to every tree in the forest.

This is how it works for you and me. Adam was the original apple that multiplied to create the forest of the human race. Every single one of us, you and myself included, is born after the template Adam broke when he sinned. He took sin inside himself and altered his nature. He changed, at the DNA level, from the image of God to the image of sin. We now bear that broken template.

A Lost Dominion

What about our dominion? That was lost, too.

As soon as Adam and Eve submitted to Satan's suggestion to eat the fruit, they put him in the place of authority in their lives. The relationship with God that was supposed to provide them with identity and direction was usurped by the devil. Now, rather than being fathered by God, they had submitted themselves to the leadership of Satan. Along with that came the keys to the authority—or dominion—God had given them. The dominion delegated to Adam and Eve was now handed over to Satan until such a time as it could be reclaimed.

Before I continue, notice what I just said: Satan procured *real* authority on the earth as a result of the Fall. When Adam and Eve sinned, their rule over the earth did not default to God. It was handed to Satan.

In my experience, many believers are confused about this and believe God retained authority over the earth throughout the events of the Old Testament. But for this to be the case, God would have had to violate the structure He had set up. When He gave authority to Adam and Eve, He *gave* it to them, for good or for bad. If they chose to use it poorly and give it away, that was their choice—otherwise, they never really had authority in the first place.

Think of it this way. Suppose I gave you my car as a gift, and you decided you wanted to paint it a color I did not like. If I took it back and did not let you do that, I never gave you my car in the first place, did I?

In the same way, Adam and Eve either had the authority God gave to them or they did not—and we know they did. When they submitted to Satan's instructions instead of God's, they placed their authority under him. He, in a real way, then became the resident ruling authority on the earth. From that point forward, he began to use that dominion on the earth the way he wanted—and what he wanted was in opposition to God's plans and will on the earth.

Jesus acknowledged this and spoke with matter-of-fact clarity about it. The Son of God called Satan the "ruler of this world" multiple times:

"Now is the judgment of this world; now will the ruler of this world be cast out."

John 12:31

"I will no longer talk much with you, for the ruler of this world is coming. He has no claim on me."

John 14:30

In the temptation in the desert, we see how far this authority goes:

And the devil took him up and showed him all the kingdoms of the world in a moment of time, and said to him, "To you I will give all this authority and their glory, for it has been delivered to me, and I give it to whom I will. If you, then, will worship me, it will all be yours."

Luke 4:5–7

Now, of course we know Satan is the father of lies. But in case you are tempted to dismiss his statement because of that, I suggest this would not have qualified as a *true* temptation if it was not a legitimate offer. All the temptations Jesus experienced were true options He could have taken.

A Broken Relationship

As I have already pointed out, there has not been much discussion thus far of sinful actions—sins that need forgiveness. The need for forgiveness exists in a third area where the original plan goes astray: the relationship between God and mankind.

Before sin entered the story, there was intimacy and relationship between God and Adam and Eve. In fact, God formed

Adam and Eve in a deeply personal way: with His own hands. After shaping Adam, the Scripture says God breathed His breath into Adam and he came to life (see Genesis 2:7). This is such a personal and intimate act of creation. God shared life with Adam with a kiss. Later, God took a rib out of Adam's side and used it to form Eve, again with His own hands. Both Adam and Eve were made through touch. God was the first being they experienced.

The text indicates God would walk and talk with them in the Garden. But when sin entered the story, this fellowship broke down:

> And they heard the sound of the LORD God walking in the garden in the cool of the day, and the man and his wife hid themselves from the presence of the LORD God among the trees of the garden. But the LORD God called to the man and said to him, "Where are you?" And he said, "I heard the sound of you in the garden, and I was afraid, because I was naked, and I hid myself."
>
> Genesis 3:8–10

As Adam and Eve hid from God, the relationship broke down. Rather than experiencing God's presence as love and freedom, shame and fear tainted the relationship. God sent them from the Garden in order to protect them, so they would not eat of the Tree of Life and live eternally as fallen creatures.

It is in this third area, the relationship between God and mankind, that forgiveness is required. We will return to this part of the story in more detail in chapter 7.

In summary, we discover three major strands were affected by the Fall:

- **Human nature:** Sin violated humanity's created purpose by twisting us into its image, instead of the image of God.

- **Cosmic authority:** Satan usurped humanity as the ruler of the created order on earth.
- **Relationship between God and mankind:** Sin created a relational divide between humanity and God.

The cosmic question coming out of Genesis 3 is this: What will God do about this? Surely Satan will not get the upper hand on God. How will God fix not only the relationship between us and Him, but also the violence done to our identity and the dominion Satan pilfered from us? That is the true question on the table.

What happened at the Fall is the bad news. With that, we turn to the good news.

THINKING LIKE JESUS

- When Adam and Eve fell, a multifold problem was introduced into the world.
- Humanity's original identity was to carry the image and likeness of God. This was lost at the Fall, as humans became sinners.
- Humanity's original destiny was to have the dominion of God on earth. This was also lost at the Fall, as Satan became the ruler of this world.
- Humanity was made to walk in relationship and intimacy with God, but sinful actions create relational breakdown between God and us.

The True Gospel

Did you know that for more than one hundred years, California was depicted as an island on maps?[1] Discovering and charting new lands is always a chaotic process and involves redacting and revising previous versions of charts. But the story of California as an island is one that illustrates the power of our own lenses.

The story begins with cartographers getting the geography correct at the onset. In 1539, Francisco de Ulloa discovered the Bay of California. Original maps, drawn in the late 1500s, showed California as the west coast of the continent, with Baja California as a southward-jutting peninsula.

However, in 1602, Sebastián Vizcaíno and Father Antonio de la Ascensión sailed up the California coast and returned with a journal of their voyage. In this journal, Ascensión asserted that Baja California was an island, separated from the American continent by what he called the Mediterranean Sea of California. It is unclear where the error came in, save that these voyagers must not have sailed up the entirety of the coast. In any case, maps began to be drafted with this new information.

California was depicted as an island with a strait running north, all the way up the inside of the Baja California peninsula to the border between the United States and Canada.

In the late 1600s, Father Eusebio Kino, a Jesuit missionary, led inland mission journeys to Baja California, planting missions along the way. When they encountered famine, they were forced to return to Mexico City. The path he traced was the first conclusive proof that California was not an island.

By the early 1700s, there had been many other journeys, and it was well documented that Baja California could not possibly be an island. Here is the amazing part of this story: The mapmakers decided to keep drawing it as an island *anyway*. They had the data to prove it was not an island, but the idea of California as an island had become ingrained into everyone's thinking. The notion that it was not an island was dismissed outright as something "everyone knows isn't true," even though it clearly was true—and there was proof!

For the first half of the eighteenth century, Baja California was intentionally drawn incorrectly as an island, just because it could not be true that anything else was possible. People had been locked in so powerfully by their lenses that they only saw what they were used to seeing, even though there was clear proof otherwise.

The story finally ended when King Ferdinand VII of Spain issued a royal edict declaring California connected to the continent of North America and, hence, not an island. Shortly after that, the "Island of California" began to disappear from maps.

The Power of Our Lenses

It seems hardest to see an issue from a new perspective when we have a perspective we are accustomed to using. When we already know what we are looking for, we tend to see what we have always seen. Our minds adapt to the lines we have established, and we find it hard to see things differently. Our perspective becomes synonymous with truth in our minds, even if it is factually wrong.

Jesus addresses this dynamic in His conclusion to the Parable of the Rich Man and Lazarus. At the end of the parable, the rich man begs Abraham to send Lazarus to warn his family of their impending torment in the afterlife. Abraham replies that they have warning enough in Moses and the Prophets. The rich man reasons that his family would listen if someone came from the dead to warn them. Abraham's response unnerves me a little bit:

> "If they do not hear Moses and the Prophets, neither will they be convinced if someone should rise from the dead."
>
> Luke 16:31

This is a powerful statement about the power of our lenses! If our lens is powerful enough to block us from seeing truth in Scripture, we are blind enough to miss the truth, even if someone were to be resurrected and share its truth with us.

This is, of course, exactly what happened to the religious leaders who hardened their hearts against Jesus and eventually crucified Him. Jesus was not the Messiah they expected. He could not possibly be. He hung out with tax collectors and prostitutes. And He healed people on the Sabbath, too. Never mind His amazing miracles or the great authority with which He taught the things of God—those were just small details. There was no way He could be the Messiah.

Our lenses, indeed, are powerful. They can make our minds run on automatic tracks that bypass the truth right in front of us. As we consider how the Gospel solves the problems raised in the last chapter—the loss of identity and dominion, as well as relationship—I would like to suggest that you keep in mind the power of your lenses about what the Gospel "should be." If we are discussing things that "couldn't possibly be the Good News," take care not to dismiss what may be the truth right in front of you. Our lenses are powerful because often they operate on an emotional level, making us cling to what we believe. From what I have discovered, what we believe about God is where it comes out more than anywhere else.

The Answer to Our Problem

The Gospel must be the answer to humanity's truest problem. We know that Satan is inferior to God. In the end, God will be victorious over the work of the enemy, and the means of His victory is the Gospel. As such, the Gospel must be God's solution to Satan's plans. This means the Gospel must go further than the forgiveness of sins because, as we saw in the last chapter, our sin actions are a symptom of our indwelling sin image.

Forgiveness of sins must be included in the Good News, yes. But the root is deeper than that, and the Gospel must address the root. Otherwise, what deals with the core of humanity's problem? What deals with the sin living in us? What deals with the restoration of our rule on the earth? If it's not the Gospel, what is it?

The fact is, many of us think the story of the Scriptures does not address these issues. We believe the Gospel is our Band-Aid—that it patches up the relationship between ourselves and God but that those deeper issues will be dealt with when we pass on from this world to the next. We will have freedom from the sin part of our being in heaven, we say. God's rule through humanity will be restored in heaven, we say.

If that is what we believe, then the Gospel is not the answer to the real issues—and I have a problem with that. I have a problem with the idea that the Good News is a temporary fix until God makes everything better. Didn't Jesus pay a high enough price to deal with the real issues in the first place? Why do we believe God's power in the afterlife is more effective than God's power through Jesus now?

I am convinced the Gospel must address the real issues right now. Otherwise, we effectively look to our own death to complete what Jesus started. When Jesus hung on the cross and with some of His last breaths uttered, "It is finished," He did not mean for us to supplement that with ". . . once we die, as well."

So, we are going to proceed on the premise that Jesus came to deal, once and for all, with what went wrong in the Garden. In fact, John tells us this is true:

> The reason the Son of God appeared was to destroy the works of the devil.
>
> 1 John 3:8

That means the Gospel must address the issues of identity and dominion, in addition to the issue of forgiveness of sins. To see how that works, we must look more closely at Scripture.

The Message of the Kingdom

As we discussed earlier, Jesus carried and preached during His life and ministry on the earth two thousand years ago the message of the Kingdom of God. He heralded this call from His earliest days of ministry until His parting words with the disciples. He preached the Kingdom at hand and taught how it worked. He demonstrated its reality with signs and wonders, and then He passed the ministry of the Kingdom to His followers on His departure:

> "You are those who have stayed with me in my trials, and I assign to you, as my Father assigned to me, a kingdom."
>
> Luke 22:28–29

This message of the Kingdom of God is to be the torch the Church carries to the ends of the earth:

> "And this gospel of the kingdom will be proclaimed throughout the whole world as a testimony to all nations, and then the end will come."
>
> Matthew 24:14

To see how this fits into the broader narrative of Scripture, let's look at a few things more closely. First, note the wording of Jesus' message, as described in His initial preaching in the book of Mark:

> "The time is fulfilled, and the kingdom of God is at hand; repent and believe in the gospel."
>
> Mark 1:15

Notice that Jesus put together two ideas: that a time had been fulfilled and that the Kingdom of God was at hand. In other words, there was a time when the Kingdom of God was *not* at hand, and Jesus' message was about the ending of that portion of time. It marked a turning point in history. Before Jesus, the Kingdom of God was not within reach. With Jesus, it now was. This framing almost sounds like Jesus is providing the answer to a question: "At last, the answer has arrived—the Kingdom of God is here!"

What question was Jesus answering with the arrival of the Kingdom of God? The answer is the dominion question that was raised in the Garden. Remember, Satan had procured the authority God had granted to Adam and Eve to have dominion over the earth. Jesus was here to bring dominion back into the hands of humanity. This is part of the reason He had to come not only as God, but as a man. Jesus was the completion of that promise given once upon a time, at the creation of humanity.

To see this more clearly, let's look at what the concept of *kingdom*, in relation to the Kingdom of God, actually means. In English, we largely associate the word *kingdom* with a noun—namely, a place. We think of the United Kingdom, a geographical region defined by the extent of land ruled by the British monarchy. Just as that is true, we tend to think of the Kingdom of God as a place, as well—sort of an analog of "God's country," so to speak.

But that was not how the Jews of Jesus' day used the term *kingdom*. For them, it was not a region but an action. It was an event, not a place. We see this in the language Jesus uses to refer to the Kingdom of God. In the Lord's Prayer, He teaches the disciples to pray:

> "Your kingdom come, your will be done, on earth as it is in heaven."
>
> Matthew 6:10

Jesus is referring to the *act* of God ruling, not the place where God rules. He is saying, "Pray that God's will is done right here, right now, the same way it is in heaven. Just like God's Word is perfectly carried out in heaven, pray the same happens on earth. That's what His kingdom coming looks like."

Another clear example happens after Jesus delivers a man from a demon. He says:

> "But if it is by the Spirit of God that I cast out demons, then the kingdom of God has come upon you."
>
> Matthew 12:28

Jesus is saying here that if the Holy Spirit, through Jesus, is driving demons out, then God is enforcing His will—His kingdom has come. God's will is being carried out in that moment.

This is the message of the Kingdom of God: that God is acting like a king and ruling again. The Kingdom of God may be better conveyed as "the kinging of God." God rules as king, not in an abstract, overall kind of way, but as a direct, in-the-moment kind of way.

With this understanding, it becomes clear that Jesus' message that the Kingdom of God is at hand is the message of the restoration of the lost dominion Satan had procured for himself. God is back on the throne, ruling through humanity again, as He always planned to do.

The Message of Righteousness

When Jesus touches down on earth and introduces the message of the Kingdom of God, we see an explosion of Kingdom activity around Him. He begins to release the Kingdom of God in signs, wonders and miracles in escalating momentum, first through Himself and eventually through His 12 apostles and, later, the 72. Everywhere they went, they carried this same message of the Kingdom of God, and the same miraculous proof followed them.

Yet for all the incredible activity that happened, Kingdom activity was still severely limited on a global scale. When Jesus was on the earth and ministering to people, the Kingdom of God did not break out in Africa, Asia or the Americas. It was not active in Europe. In fact, it was released only in Israel.

More specifically, it was only connected to Jesus. It migrated one step away from Him through His followers. However, only people who knew Jesus and had a relationship with Him were drawn into His mission and able to carry the message of the Kingdom of God and its accompanying power. The Kingdom of God, in other words, was tied to the person of Jesus alone. This is because Jesus was the only One who could say the following:

> "Have I been with you so long, and you still do not know me, Philip? Whoever has seen me has seen the Father. How can you say, 'Show us the Father'?"
>
> John 14:9

"Whoever has seen me has seen the Father . . ." What does that sound like to you? It sounds to me like Jesus is claiming to be the image of God! Of course, we know He is the visible image of the invisible God (see Colossians 1:15), but often we connect that to the incarnation and miss the fact that in Jesus, we see the example of what humanity was supposed to be.

Jesus is the image of God and carries the message of the dominion of God. He truly is the second Adam. He was born of a virgin and, as such, did not carry the nature of fallen man, but rather the nature bestowed by His Father in heaven, as spoken in Genesis 1:26.

As with all of creation, doing comes out of being. This is why the image of God was assigned first—because out of the image of God, Adam and Eve were to rule. Jesus coming to restore the Kingdom of God on earth requires restoring the image of God to humanity as well, so we can rule from that identity and release the Kingdom.

To that end, Jesus does something shocking: He goes to the cross and dies. Three days later, He resurrects. As we will see in more detail in the next few chapters, this happens not just to forgive our sins, but also to remove our sin identity. His death and resurrection made a new thing possible: the restoration of the image of God to humanity. This is what Scripture refers to as righteousness.

Righteousness is another unfortunate word, as it is a relatively archaic term. I have never heard it used, outside of slang, in a nonreligious context. It generally winds up becoming a "Bible word" that does not mean a whole lot to many of us. If you ask around, you will find pastors who can define it for you, often using the language "right standing before God." In my opinion, that is not a very accessible definition.

Let's look up what the word means. *Thayer's Greek Lexicon* defines *righteousness* this way:

1. in a broad sense: state of him who is as he ought to be, righteousness, the condition acceptable to God
   a. the doctrine concerning the way in which man may attain a state approved of God
   b. integrity, virtue, purity of life, rightness, correctness of thinking, feeling, and acting
2. in a narrower sense, justice or the virtue which gives each his due

Look at the first definition, which gives its primary meaning. Righteousness is the "state of him who is as he ought to be." In other words, righteousness means *right in being*. It means you are what you are supposed to be, not what you are not supposed to be. The biblical contrast to the term *righteous* is the term *sinner*:

For as by the one man's disobedience the many were made sinners, so by the one man's obedience the many will be made righteous.

Romans 5:19

This verse sums up the identity narrative in Scripture. Adam disobeyed and broke the essence of who we were supposed to be, making us sinners, and Jesus came to fix that and set it straight, restoring us to righteousness.

What does this mean? It means those of us in Christ have been restored to the image and likeness of God! This statement may seem too grandiose to be true, but it is exactly how Paul describes the new creation we are in Jesus:

Put on the new self, created after the likeness of God in true righteousness and holiness.

Ephesians 4:24

Jesus' life, death and resurrection deal with the problems introduced at the Fall.

	Image and Likeness of God	Dominion of God
Creation	Given to humanity to represent God to the created order	Entrusted to humanity to continue to conform this planet to God's design
The Fall	Replaced by the image of sin and revealed in our sinful actions	Traded away to Satan when Adam and Eve submitted to his counsel
Jesus	Came to us as the visible image of the invisible God	Demonstrated God's rule as He restored through healing, deliverance and ministry
Gospel Language	Righteousness by faith	Kingdom of God

With this framework in mind, a few things begin to make a lot more sense. For example, consider one of the questions we had in chapter 2: Do Jesus and Paul speak different messages? No, they do not, because the Good News is not the Kingdom *or* righteousness. It is Jesus. Jesus is the Good News. Mark tells us:

> The beginning of the gospel of Jesus Christ, the Son of God.
>
> Mark 1:1

What comes to us in the person of Jesus is righteousness (through His death and resurrection) and the Kingdom of God (through His life and His coming as the King of the Kingdom). In the truest sense, both Jesus and Paul talked about what Jesus did. Jesus told us what He was doing through His life, and Paul picked up that message and clarified what became available to us through Jesus' death and resurrection. They both make clear that Jesus brought us the solution to both issues facing humanity:

> "But seek first the kingdom of God and his righteousness, and all these things will be added to you."
>
> Matthew 6:33

> For I decided to know nothing among you except Jesus Christ [Jesus, the Messiah—the one anointed to bring the Kingdom of God] and him crucified [opening up to us righteousness by faith through His crucifixion and resurrection].
>
> 1 Corinthians 2:2

The Message of Forgiveness

Let's turn back to the question of forgiveness now. If Jesus' death and resurrection make us a new creation, where does that leave us with forgiveness? Are our sins forgiven at the cross? To this, Scripture says a wholehearted *yes*:

> And every priest stands daily at his service, offering repeatedly the same sacrifices, which can never take away sins. *But when Christ had offered for all time a single sacrifice for sins*, he sat down at the right hand of God.
>
> Hebrews 10:11–12, emphasis mine

Scripture says Jesus offered Himself as the sacrifice for our sins. He was the sin sacrifice we each needed to be forgiven.

Even in affirming this, we begin to see that if our picture stops here, it is incomplete. In fact, the writer of Hebrews indicates that the ministry of forgiveness is not as good as what Jesus extends to us:

> But as it is, Christ has obtained a ministry that is as much more excellent than the old as the covenant he mediates is better, since it is enacted on better promises.
>
> Hebrews 8:6

Now, do not get me wrong. Forgiveness is amazing! I am not saying I am not grateful for it or that forgiveness would not be enough of a gift in the Gospel to make me thrilled. I am simply pointing out that Scripture indicates the ministry of Jesus is "more excellent" than the ministry of forgiveness that was possible in the Old Covenant. Why? Because the New Covenant gives us better promises—the promises of righteousness and the Kingdom, *in addition to* the promise of forgiveness.

I cannot help but wonder if our problem with the Gospel is that we have majored on such a small portion of what is available. We have excluded much of what it really is. We have focused on forgiveness to the exclusion of the depths of righteousness or what is available in the Kingdom of God. No wonder we seem to hit a ceiling in our faith or feel like things are not working the way Scripture says they should.

Here, we see a big shift. How are we to understand this radical new suggestion concerning the Gospel—that it contains more than just forgiveness and, in actuality, restores to us the identity and dominion we lost at the Fall?

It can surely cause us uncertainty and fear to consider shifting the core of our faith so significantly. What gives me the boldness to even suggest such a thing is the fruit of the journey—the fruit Scripture speaks of. It is hard to argue with people falling more in love with Jesus, loving others around them more deeply, pursuing worship and the Scriptures with a passion and living out their faith with greater clarity and conviction. And that is to say nothing of being empowered to share their faith and access the supernatural power of the Kingdom!

In the last few years, I have witnessed this fruit at work in my church, where we have been on the same journey of understanding described in these pages. Dianne Leman and her husband, Happy, have pastored our church since they founded it in the late 1970s. Since that time, the church has grown from a small group that gathered in their home to thousands spread throughout central Illinois.

This journey God was preparing and unveiling to us was punctuated by a visit from an evangelist named Todd White. Here is Dianne's account of the fruit of the Spirit that has changed our perspective on the Gospel:

> "I've been sent by God to drop a bomb," the dreadlocked evangelist soberly announced to the 970 people sitting in the Vineyard Church auditorium.
>
> My heart sank as visions of churchwide destruction flashed before my eyes. My husband and I were (and still are) the senior

pastors of those intent listeners, and my shepherd's heart quaked with fear. Bombs were not typically a good thing!

"Yes," the guest speaker continued, "God wants revival—a revival of righteousness—and it begins in each of you."

A revival of righteousness? I had no idea what those words meant. But in my heart—the same heart that had moments ago quaked with fear—faith was ignited by the Holy Spirit, and I knew God had spoken. I humbled my heart and mind to receive.

So began the most exhilarating and the most challenging adventure of our almost forty years of ministry. It was January 2012, and ever since, the Holy Spirit has been leading us as a church community into all truth—the truth of the Gospel, the whole Gospel of who we are in Christ and His glorious grace toward us.

We have had to put on "Gospel glasses" so we can see things differently, and this has not always been easy. But despite a few angry "sheep," some skepticism and fear of deception, we have never once questioned the Holy Spirit's work in our lives. We were blind, but now we see. We now see things in the Scriptures that we never really saw before, when we viewed with our old paradigm.

A true revival of righteousness has broken out, and the glorious Gospel has gotten clearer and clearer. The litmus test for us has been that month after month, we see Jesus—bigger, better and more beautiful than ever. And those intent listeners, those precious people we lead and pastor, have likewise had their eyes opened and their lives transformed as we learn to embrace Jesus' righteousness as our own. God gives grace to the humble.

It can be scary to adjust our understanding of the Gospel, but the fruit speaks for itself. I have seen too many lives transformed to consider any other road right now. There was a time I was ashamed of the Gospel, but I can be ashamed no longer. I have seen God's power for salvation for everyone who believes.

Through faith, God gives us righteousness and we begin a whole new journey—one that was always purposed for us. How does that happen? We turn to that question next.

THINKING LIKE JESUS

- The problems introduced by the Fall are addressed by the Gospel.
- The lost identity of the image and likeness of God was renewed through the death and resurrection of Jesus and restored to us through the righteousness by faith Jesus offers us.
- The lost destiny of the dominion of God was restored as Jesus came, bringing the Kingdom of God, and as He defeated the devil and drafts us into continuing the ministry of the Kingdom.

5

You Are Not What You Used to Be

One of my good friends, Brad Hart, has a photography business. God has gifted him with an incredible eye to capture not just the beauty of a moment, but also the emotion of it. He gets bookings all over the country to shoot weddings, engaged couples, births, families and more.

As Brad has undertaken this venture, I have been struck by how much his creativity is tied to who he is. As I look through his photos, I am moved by how much I see *him* in them. No, he does not take photos of himself, but I can look at one of his photographs and think, *That one is so Brad.*

That is such a strange thing to think. How is a photo like Brad? I am not sure how it works, but I recognize a certain vibe, style and feel to his photos that are the same vibe and feel I get in his presence. Something of Brad is in his art.

From this, we know there is something deeply personal about the creative process. No matter the way we create, we pour something of ourselves into it. This is why it hurts when people critique what we have created. They criticize not only the quality of what we have produced, but our very selves.

The same is true when it comes to God's creative work. God is the Creator, and we are the created. He is a masterful artist, and in creating us, He not only designed us well, but also poured who He is into us.

At some point, though, it became pious to degrade humanity in an attempt to glorify God. We think of ourselves as lowly to try to show how great God is—that He is nothing like us, that He exists on an echelon above our meager and flawed human existence.

But think about this. If I were to critique Brad's photos in an attempt to build him up, I doubt he would feel uplifted. Imagine if I said, "That photo is terrible. You're way better than that photo. I'm so glad you have nothing in common with that lousy print." How do you think Brad would feel as a result? He poured himself into that photo. It contains an element of his essence. To say it is terrible is to critique him, too.

Rather than divide the photo and the photographer, a more uplifting response to the creator's work would be to say, "I really like this one. Not only did you capture the moment, but I see you in it, as well."

When it comes to our humanity, we should start from this understanding. This is, in essence, the starting point of Scripture. We see God as the Creator and ourselves as the pinnacle of His creation. Ephesians 2:10 tells us, "For we are his workmanship."

If that is how God sees us, it needs to become the way we see ourselves. But people often create a façade of how they believe God sees them—that they are broken and messed up but God sees them through some kind of "Jesus glasses" that filter out all the bad stuff and present a rose-colored picture of who they are.

That kind of thinking is not helpful. It is tantamount to saying God's view of reality is distorted and inaccurate. We seem to be conveying we understand ourselves better than God does, that somehow He is a bit confused about who we really are.

It is more likely that if God and I do not agree on who I am, then I am the one whose views are distorted. If He sees me differently than I see myself, that means my perception is wrong and I need to let Him adjust my view. When the way I see myself is how He sees me, I have come into a place of truth.

Think about it through the lens of pride and humility. Most of us define *pride* as "thinking highly of ourselves" and *humility* as "thinking lowly of ourselves." If that is the case, and since we are supposed to be humble, then we minimize our good qualities and focus on the areas in which we still have a long way to go.

This is the opposite of what we intuitively know is healthy. No parent would raise his or her children that way and expect them to succeed in life. We encourage our children, point out what they do well and draw their focus toward those things. We coach them deeper into who they are. We bolster the good we see in them and promote their development. We encourage them to improve in the areas outside their strengths. Most of all, we reinforce their sense of value and our love for them. We help them form a view of themselves that is in alignment with the way we see them.

We would do well to adopt a similar posture when it comes to our relationship with God. We are His children, and He is raising us to see ourselves through His eyes. It is not prideful to agree with the good things God sees in us, and it is not humble to dismiss those good things or to pretend they are not there. True humility is admitting God knows us better than we know ourselves. It is realizing that when He looks at us, He sees us more clearly than we can see ourselves. It is allowing our self-perception to be molded by Him. The heart of humility is a self-view in submission to God, admitting that He is the potter and we are the clay. As His vessels, we accept that if God desires to lift us up, it is His right to do so.

So, how does God see us? As we discovered in the last chapter, God now sees us as righteous. The biblical word *righteousness* is an identity word. It describes who we are in Christ. It refers to our state of being. Specifically, it means *right in being*—that we are who we are supposed to be. Since we are supposed to carry the image and likeness of God, that means righteousness, for us, is being in the image and likeness of God (see Colossians 3:10; Ephesians 4:24).

I know that seems like an extreme thing to say. We are in the image and likeness of God? How on earth can that be? We will look at how that happens in just a moment, but let me first clear away two common questions that pop up at this point.

The first thought many of us have when we consider an idea like that is how incredibly prideful it sounds. How could we possibly say we are carrying God's image? As I previously mentioned, true humility is submitting to God's definition of us. I am not saying *I* think you carry the image of God. I am saying *God* says that. I agree it sounds too good to be true—and maybe that is why it requires faith to believe it. But if God says that is who we are, submission to that definition is true humility.

The other question that comes up at this point refers to sin. If we are made in the image of God, why do we still sin? Why do we still want to sin? What does that mean? That is a great question, and we will dive into it a lot more in the next chapter. For now, I would ask you to push pause with me on these questions until we get there.

We Died with Jesus

Okay, so we are righteous. We have been made right again. How does that work? Let's walk through the way Paul describes it.

In the second half of Romans 5, Paul talks about salvation. He describes how Adam fell and we were all born with a sinner identity, meaning an identity that has been broken by sin. He says Jesus came to offer us a new identity in Him—a righteous one. God, through His grace, offers us the free gift of righteousness through Jesus.

Then in the first half of Romans 6, Paul turns to how that salvation works. Here is what he says:

> Do you not know that all of us who have been baptized into Christ Jesus were baptized into his death? We were buried therefore with him by baptism into death, in order that, just as Christ was raised from the dead by the glory of the Father, we too might walk in newness of life.
>
> Romans 6:3–4

Paul says those of us who are baptized into Christ Jesus were baptized into His death, so that when Jesus was resurrected, we joined Him in new life. This might seem a little bizarre, but the term *baptize* was a metaphorical term that did not necessarily have a religious connotation at the time Paul was writing. The word simply means something along the lines of "being immersed." My understanding is that you would "baptize" a cloth into dye to color it or "baptize" a cucumber in brine to turn it into a pickle. So, when Paul is saying we were baptized into Jesus' death, he is saying that just as we immerse ourselves in water, we were immersed into Christ's death when He died. We were brought into death with Him, so that we could be brought into new life with Him when He resurrected.

This is a major shift in our understanding of the Gospel. Paul is not saying Jesus died *for* us. He is saying that Jesus died *as* us. Furthermore, he is saying we died with Jesus and resurrected with Him, as well. In fact, Paul continues to expound on that analogy by saying:

> For if we have been united with him in a death like his, we shall certainly be united with him in a resurrection like his.
>
> Romans 6:5

Paul introduces his reasoning by explaining that we are united with Jesus in death and resurrection. This is such a change! Jesus did not just die for us; we died with Him.

I do not know about you, but for a long time I missed that Paul comes back to this over and over again as the core of the Gospel. Let me show you a few other places this comes up:

> I have been crucified with Christ. It is no longer I who live, but Christ who lives in me. And the life I now live in the flesh I live by faith in the Son of God, who loved me and gave himself for me.
>
> Galatians 2:20

> And you, who were dead in your trespasses and the uncircumcision of your flesh, God made alive together with him, having forgiven us all our trespasses.
>
> Colossians 2:13

> But God, being rich in mercy, because of the great love with which he loved us, even when we were dead in our trespasses, made us alive together with Christ—by grace you have been saved—and raised us up with him and seated us with him in the heavenly places in Christ Jesus.
>
> Ephesians 2:4–6

Notice the language Paul uses in these verses, which is also used in many other places in his letters. For Paul, death and resurrection happen along with Jesus and in Jesus. Again, this is not language about Jesus dying for us but about us dying with Jesus.

What does this dying with Jesus and resurrecting with Jesus mean? Let's continue in the Romans 6 passage:

> We know that our old self was crucified with him in order that the body of sin might be brought to nothing, so that we would no longer be enslaved to sin. For one who has died has been set free from sin.
>
> Romans 6:6–7

Here, Paul says we were crucified with Jesus so we would be set free from sin. Our captivity to sin is broken, and sin is brought to nothing in us. This is a big deal! Paul is saying that when Jesus hung on the cross, the sinful us—the person who had sin living at the core—hung on the cross with Him. That person died along with Jesus.

Let me make this concrete. However negatively we see ourselves—as a sinner, loser, failure, sell-out, outsider, reject, burden, has-been or anything else—all of that hung with Jesus on the cross and died. That person is no longer who we are. You are not a loser. You are not a failure. You are not worthless or rejected. You *were* those things, because that is what sin did to us. It broke us at the *being* level. We had not just *done* wrong; we *were* wrong. *Wrong* became our identity. But Jesus took that wrong being upon Himself, and that wrong being died and was buried in the tomb.

What becomes of us, then? Paul tells us:

> Now if we have died with Christ, we believe that we will also live with him. We know that Christ, being raised from the dead, will never die again; death no longer has dominion over him.

For the death he died he died to sin, once for all, but the life he lives he lives to God.

Romans 6:8–10

Because we have been joined with Jesus in His death, we also join with Him in resurrection. In fact, we have been born again as a new creation. We are not who we were. We are wholly new. Likewise, we walk out of the tomb with Jesus on the far side of the fall of this creation.

Jesus died for sin, once and for all, and it is not on His mind anymore. That means sin has been dealt with. Now Jesus is focused on living to God. Likewise, we have been made alive to God, and sin has been killed in us. We have died to sin, once and for all, too, and now we live unto God.

Again, this is so different from how we usually think of ourselves. My default is to see myself through the lens of my failures or disappointments and to assign myself that identity. I tend to think of myself as still working through issues and wrestling with sin. Paul says all of that is a false mindset. He says I have died to those things and that it is not who I am anymore. My journey is no longer one of dying to sin but of being alive to God.

Just in case that thought seems a little off-base, notice the next verse, which is the first thing Paul instructs us to do in the whole book of Romans:

So you also must consider yourselves dead to sin and alive to God in Christ Jesus.

Romans 6:11

This is not a recommendation. It is a command! Paul tells us to consider—to spend time intentionally reflecting on—ourselves as dead to sin and alive to God in Christ Jesus. He wants us to work out what that means.

The idea that we must partner with God to form a mindset in alignment with the reality of our co-death and co-resurrection with Jesus is an important one, and one we will return to over the next few chapters. For now, I would like to offer a thought for some reflection: Do you think of yourself as dead to sin and alive to God? As we have discussed numerous times in this book, we tend to see ourselves as very much alive to sin. We expect it to be part of our lives, something we are still wrestling through. But if that is how we see ourselves, then we are disobeying Paul's command.

Our belief that we are alive to sin is often reinforced when we encounter Romans 7—a passage of Scripture often considered an example of what it looks like to be caught in a battle between our flesh and our more spiritual desires, and offered by Paul, no less. The famous passage reads:

> For we know that the law is spiritual, but I am of the flesh, sold under sin. For I do not understand my own actions. For I do not do what I want, but I do the very thing I hate. Now if I do what I do not want, I agree with the law, that it is good. So now it is no longer I who do it, but sin that dwells within me. For I know that nothing good dwells in me, that is, in my flesh. For I have the desire to do what is right, but not the ability to carry it out. For I do not do the good I want, but the evil I do not want is what I keep on doing. Now if I do what I do not want, it is no longer I who do it, but sin that dwells within me.
>
> Romans 7:14–20

What is happening here? Is Paul describing his experience of captivity to sin, even after being saved? I do not believe he is.

Instead, I believe he is building a line of reasoning that flows from chapter 6 through chapter 8.

In Romans 6, Paul describes the logic of how we are saved. In Romans 8, he teaches how we are to live in light of that. Romans 7 serves as a "gap chapter" between the two that discusses why the Law was significant. A key here is to remember that Paul was writing to a church mixed with Jews and Gentiles. He knew the Jews were going to ask why the Law mattered if salvation came through Jesus instead of the Law. To address that question, he uses the "gap chapter" of Romans 7.

This is why he introduces Romans 7 the way he does:

> Or do you not know, brothers—*for I am speaking to those who know the law*—that the law is binding on a person only as long as he lives?
>
> Romans 7:1, emphasis mine

Through the rest of the chapter, Paul makes two points: how we are no longer under the Law (see verses 1–6) and what purpose the Law served (see verses 7–25). In the second portion, Paul recalls his experience of being under the Law. He starts by pointing out it was in the past, not the present:

> The very commandment that promised life *proved* to be death to me.
>
> Romans 7:10, emphasis mine

> Did that which is good, then, bring death to me? By no means! It *was* sin, producing death in me through what is good, in order that sin might be shown to be sin, and through the commandment might become sinful beyond measure.
>
> Romans 7:13, emphasis mine

Then Paul changes to the present tense to describe his experience of wrestling with the sin nature he had while living under the Law:

> For we know that the law is spiritual, but I am of the flesh, sold under sin.
>
> Romans 7:14

Is Paul sold under sin now that he is a believer? No! He is dead to sin. He has already made clear he is no longer bound to the Law (see Romans 7:1–6) and is no longer sold under sin (see Romans 6:17–18). There was a time he *was* bound and sold, though. What was that experience like? It looked like this:

> For I do not understand my own actions. For I do not do what I want, but I do the very thing I hate.
>
> Romans 7:15

> For I do not do the good I want, but the evil I do not want is what I keep on doing.
>
> Romans 7:19

> So now it is no longer I who do it, but sin that dwells within me.
>
> Romans 7:17

This is exactly why Jesus came—so we would not have to live this way anymore and to deliver us from the bondage of the Law and our indwelling sin nature. Paul's point is that the Law was not a solution to him because it aggravated the sin nature. The Law was a mirror that showed the presence of sin dwelling within.

You may wonder why Paul uses the present tense here to describe a former struggle. Why does he make it seem he is talking about something that is still going on? I would say this has to do with the flexibility of language and the way we use language while telling stories. Consider if I told you the following: *I was walking down the road the other day, enjoying the beautiful spring air. It was such a nice day. I remember it now: I'm breathing the fresh air and humming as I'm walking down the sidewalk. My thoughts are free, and the day is wonderful. I wish every day was like that one!* I just fluidly transitioned from the past tense (describing the event) to the present tense (recalling my experience during the event) and back to the past tense (reflecting on the event). Paul's structure of language and argument follows the same path here. He describes the fact of being under the Law, then his experience while under it, then what the Law did.

So, what is Paul's ultimate conclusion? That Jesus has set us free from sin and the Law and empowered us to live in a way the Law never could:

> For God has done what the law, weakened by the flesh, could not do. By sending his own Son in the likeness of sinful flesh and for sin, he condemned sin in the flesh, in order that the righteous requirement of the law might be fulfilled in us, who walk not according to the flesh but according to the Spirit.
>
> Romans 8:3–4

We are not alive to sin; we are dead to it. Why do we still struggle? That is a fantastic question and one we will examine in depth in the next chapter. As we will see, the answer does not undermine what Paul has clearly stated: that we are dead to sin and alive to God and that we need to reckon that reality true in our lives.

Jesus Says It, Too

I know this may seem kind of scandalous. It may feel like I am suggesting our whole Gospel story is wrong. Again, I am not saying that as much as I am saying we have been missing a major piece of it. If what I am suggesting is true, then many of us are trying to live out our Christianity on a fraction of the truth. No wonder we are frustrated and it does not seem to be working!

If the process of co-death and co-resurrection with Jesus really is the picture painted in Scripture—and I would say that it is—then we should expect to see it not only in Paul's writings, but also in what Jesus said.

Indeed, we do see this same story played out in Jesus' words, as well. In John 3, we find the famous conversation Jesus shared with Nicodemus about being born again. First, though, note that the conversation begins with a connection between the Kingdom and righteousness:

> This man came to Jesus by night and said to him, "Rabbi, we know that you are a teacher come from God, for no one can do these signs that you do unless God is with him." Jesus answered him, "Truly, truly, I say to you, unless one is born again he cannot see the kingdom of God."
>
> John 3:2–3

Nicodemus opens a conversation about signs, and Jesus redirects and clarifies it, saying it is only by being born again that one can see the Kingdom of God—and, by extension, work the signs Nicodemus says are proof that God is with them. Notice the language Jesus uses: that of new birth and a complete restart.

Nicodemus is as confused as the rest of us would be. So, he and Jesus have a conversation about what it means to be born again. Jesus indicates it means being spiritually reborn.

Nicodemus asks how it is possible for someone to be spiritually reborn. This is the same question we have been considering: How does salvation work? Jesus explains:

> "If I have told you earthly things and you do not believe, how can you believe if I tell you heavenly things? No one has ascended into heaven except he who descended from heaven, the Son of Man. And as Moses lifted up the serpent in the wilderness, so must the Son of Man be lifted up, that whoever believes in him may have eternal life."
>
> John 3:12–15

Jesus first indicates He is talking about a spiritual reality, not an earthly one. This is important. We are not discussing something that will necessarily make sense to us. We are talking about a spiritual reality God unveils. It comes to us through revelation, not through knowledge.

Next, Jesus clarifies that only He has ascended into heaven. Only He is a new creation, living in alignment with the heavenly realms and partnering with them. As such, to enter into the heavenly reality of being born again in the spirit requires being connected with Him.

Jesus is building up to Nicodemus's question. At last, He addresses the process of salvation. In doing so, He references what would have been a familiar story to Nicodemus: the story of the bronze serpent recorded in Numbers 21:4–9. Jesus indicates that the way He saves us is similar to how that story played out.

I would encourage you to read that story for yourself, but I will review it here. The story opens with the Israelites complaining and speaking against God and Moses (again). As a result, God dispatches poisonous snakes, which bite the Israelites, and they begin to die. The Israelites beg Moses for help (again), and God instructs Moses to make a bronze serpent and to lift it up on a pole. Anyone who was bitten by the serpents and looked to the pole would live.

Jesus refers to this story and indicates that the salvation He provides works the same way as that of the bronze serpent that was lifted up to save the Israelites. Jesus is saying that we are like the Israelites who were bitten by poisonous serpents. Our serpent was the original serpent in the Garden, and the poison of the Fall has afflicted us all. Jesus provides salvation by becoming the serpent (He becomes sin) that is lifted up on the pole (the cross). As we look to Him on the pole, we are saved from the poison of the Fall.

The key idea is that Jesus is lifted up as sin on the cross. It is rather amazing. Jesus uses death to kill sin, and when we look to Him in faith, we are joined in that reality. Sin in us is killed.

He Became Sin for Us

Jesus not only explains how salvation works, but He also lives this out in His journey from the Last Supper to Calvary. In John 17, He prays just before He begins the journey from Gethsemane to Calvary:

> "I do not ask for these only, but also for those who will believe in me through their word, that they may all be one, just as you, Father, are in me, and I in you, that they also may be in us, so that the world may believe that you have sent me."
>
> John 17:20–21

Jesus asks that everyone who believes in Him be united as one and in Him. Now, it is possible to read this prayer as metaphorical, but I think it is quite literal. Jesus is asking for anyone who believes in Him to be united with Him in that moment.

Everything that happens to Jesus from that moment on is about Him becoming one with us.

Immediately after His prayer, Jesus takes the disciples to a garden. This is another parallel—the sin problem started in a garden. Jesus endures the process of becoming sin in the same place we did. He agonizes as the burden of sin is put upon Him. He prays and asks for help, but He is left to do it alone as the disciples fall asleep.

Next, His friend Judas comes and betrays Him, giving Him over to the religious leaders. Meanwhile, the rest of the disciples flee and abandon Him. In this, we see a reflection of the way community was broken between Adam and Eve and their subsequent family, as they betrayed each other and their covenant relationship through blame and accusation.

Later, Jesus bears accusation from the religious officials. They ridicule and mock Him, eventually condemning Him to death. This is the same way Satan accuses and condemns us. In fact, Jesus earlier pointed out that the Pharisees were sons of their father, the devil (see John 8:44).

The process continues as Jesus is questioned, accused and beaten. Each deed is an element of Jesus stepping into what sin did to us. Why was He accused? To step into our accusation. Why was He beaten? Because sin marred and broke us. In fact, Isaiah says He was beaten so intensely, He could not be recognized as a man (see Isaiah 52:14). This was exactly what sin did to us. It so broke us that the original image and likeness we were meant to bear was unrecognizable. Step by step, Jesus becomes everything we were.

It culminates in Jesus being a complete and total mess. Bruised, betrayed and belittled, Jesus carries a cross—as well as He could carry it, anyway—through Jerusalem toward Calvary. This is symbolic and profound. Jesus has become sin, and He takes the very instrument of deception used against us—a tree—and brings it up the mountain, back to the beginning. (Ezekiel 28:13–14 points out that the Garden of Eden was on a mountain.)

There, on top of the mountain, God takes everything sin did to humanity and puts it back on the tree in the form of His Son. Jesus enters into everything we were and dies as us, so that His death kills sin in us and frees us from the Fall.

This is what could not be done before Jesus. This is why Jesus had to die: because only in Him could we die and be freed from the way sin strangled our humanity and left us a pathetic shadow of God's created intent for us. Paul again tells us how it is:

> For God has done what the law, weakened by the flesh, could not do. By sending his own Son in the likeness of sinful flesh and for sin, he condemned sin in the flesh.
>
> Romans 8:3

The Sacraments Reiterate This

Let me point out one more illustration of this in Scripture and in Church history. Most of the Church celebrates two sacraments that Jesus left with us: baptism and Communion. These are more than rituals. They are symbolic, indeed prophetic, acts God uses to bestow His grace upon us and make the Gospel more and more real to us. They do not save us in themselves, but they offer a path for our salvation to continue to grow into fullness.

Both of these sacraments exist to point to and reinforce the salvation story. First, let's consider Communion (see Luke 22:14–23). At Communion, Jesus first offers the disciples some bread, saying it is His body, broken for them. What is He doing? He is identifying that He is going to be broken and that the breaking of His body is happening for them. Notice what happens next, though. He asks the disciples to eat it. He does not just break the bread; He breaks the bread and tells the disciples to take His very body inside themselves.

Here, again, we have an intentional parallel to the Fall. There was an earlier time when eating something—a piece of fruit—resulted in a change in nature. Jesus took that same process and redeemed it. The end of the story is no longer that Adam and Eve ate the fruit in the Garden but that we have eaten of Jesus, which changes our nature to match His.

Furthermore, Jesus says the cup is about the blood He is going to shed to create a New Covenant. We are going to be united with Jesus not only in His brokenness but all the way through to a New Covenant. This points to redemption—the New Covenant the prophets Jeremiah and Ezekiel prophesied about (see Jeremiah 31:31–34; Ezekiel 36:26–32), where we would be given a new heart and a new spirit and be made a new creation in Him.

So, Communion is all about being made one with Jesus, joined with His body in its brokenness and in His redemption, as well. But what about baptism? Paul explains it this way:

In him also you were circumcised with a circumcision made without hands, by putting off the body of the flesh, by the circumcision of Christ, having been buried with him in baptism, in which you were also raised with him through faith in the powerful working of God, who raised him from the dead.

Colossians 2:11–12

In baptism, we celebrate that we are joined with Jesus in burial (going under the water) and resurrection (coming out of the water). This corresponds to a spiritual circumcision—cutting away the "body of the flesh," an analogy for our sinful nature—and coming into new life with Jesus.

Baptism is a physical acting out of a spiritual reality. As we experience baptism, the part of us that learns experientially comes in touch with the cosmic reality that we have died and been buried with Jesus and that as we are resurrected with Him, we are made new.

You Are Made New

In this chapter, we have discussed one theme over and over: We died and were resurrected along with Jesus. As a result, the sin that lived within us has been killed, and we have been birthed again into new life. We are now restored to what we were first created to be.

We have looked at this several different ways because it is the central element of salvation in Scripture: *You are not just forgiven; you are free—free from what sin did to you.*

In the next few chapters, we will examine what that means and how it plays out in our lives, but this has to become an anchor point. You are not who you were. You are not defined by sin any longer. You are defined by Jesus now. To think otherwise is to disagree with God.

For many of us, this means a big change. When I teach this message, I am often struck by how uncomfortable believers are with seeing themselves as dead to sin. The unfortunate reality is that most of us have built an identity of ourselves as sinners. We see ourselves as losers and failures. To be anything else throws us into an identity crisis.

If we see ourselves through sin, that means we have faith in the idea of our sinfulness. That faith not only stands in contradiction to the Gospel, but also gets lived out in our actions. No wonder so many of us struggle to break free of the feeling that we wrestle and struggle with sin! To do anything else is to lose track of who we think we are.

There is a better way. It may not be comfortable, but I encourage you to allow the Holy Spirit to begin to cast off the self-image you have built around yourself as a sinner and to allow Him to give you a new identity—an identity rooted in your union with Christ, in being joined with Him in death and resurrection, in being saved from sin and alive to God. Yield your self-definition to His direction, and allow Him to tell you who you are: *You are not who you think you are. You are who He says you are.*

This is true repentance, where we not only forsake sinful actions, but also forsake sin as an identity, turning to God and allowing Him to establish an identity in us.

This shift in understanding changes our experience of life. When this sinks in and becomes the starting point for how we see ourselves, it provides for us the identity so many of us are searching for. When we begin to see ourselves the way God does, we are set free to live how He says we can live.

You may be saying, "That sounds awesome! How do I do that?" We will look more toward application as our journey unfolds.

THINKING LIKE JESUS

- Our lost identity is restored by being joined to Jesus in His death and resurrection. Being joined to Jesus in death means our sin nature died with Jesus on the cross. Being joined to Jesus in resurrection means we have been born again to new life, thereby restored to the identity God originally created in us.

- Co-death and co-resurrection with Jesus means we are not just forgiven. We are also free from who we used to be and free to be who God intended us to be all along.

6

A Tale
of Two Natures

Y*ou are the best of you; you are the worst of you . . .*
So begins the story most of us, as believers, carry
of ourselves. This is the picture I had growing up: that
while the good news of the Gospel had saved me, sin was still an
active force in my life and would be a source of struggle for me
until the end of my days. I was dead to sin but wrestling against
my flesh. I lived with an inner war. I wanted to live faithfully
for Jesus, but part of me resisted and required submission. It
required dying to myself daily.

Sound familiar?

Here is the problem with this picture: *It does not come from
the Bible.* Instead, it is something we project onto the Bible. This
is a common error that can happen when we process Scripture.

There are two ways we can read the Bible:

- **Exegesis (helpful):** approaching the Bible with an open
  mind and allowing Scripture to speak for itself, even if
  you do not understand or like what it says

- **Eisegesis (not helpful):** approaching the Bible with biases or presuppositions and projecting them onto Scripture so that it says what you expect it to say

In the second case, rather than letting Scripture speak for itself, we read into the text what we expect to hear. This happens because of the tension that comes from trying to reconcile our theology and our experience. We see that Scripture says we are dead to sin, but we know we struggle with temptation, failure and so on. Our theology and experience do not seem to line up, so what do we do about that?

When we come to a point of tension between theology and experience, we need to be careful how we navigate those waters. It is fair for us to require our theology to explain our experience. Truth should not deny reality, after all. But it is not okay to allow our experience to direct our theology. Once that happens, we have stepped squarely into the "not helpful" way to read Scripture, approaching the page with a bias of experience and letting that color our interpretation of what it says. Instead, we ought to keep pressing into Scripture, allowing it to form our theology until it does match up with our experience.

A Question of Death

In the matter of whether or not we are truly dead to sin, I am reminded of a humorous scene in the movie *The Princess Bride*. The main character, Westley, has died, and his two sidekicks, Inigo and Fezzik, take him to a local healer named Miracle Max to see if anything can be done. Inigo tells Max that Westley is dead, but the questionable healer says the man is only "mostly dead." It is one of many ridiculous scenes in the movie, and a memorable one because of the obvious absurdity of the idea of someone being "mostly dead."

Here's the thing: When we say we are dead to sin but that we still struggle against a part of ourselves, we are essentially saying Paul has applied the same logic to us. Either we are dead to sin or we are not. Death is a final kind of metaphor. We cannot be "mostly dead." To suggest Paul is painting that picture is to say he chose a wholly inaccurate metaphor when he said we are dead to sin.

I remember being confused by the logic of this dead-but-not-really-dead-to-sin idea in my younger years and asking what it meant. I was given the explanation that we are not completely free from sin—that its *power* has been broken, which makes it possible for us to live in freedom from it, but that it still hangs around and plays a significant part in our lives.

Now, I love the people who sought to explain this to me, and I do not want to dishonor their wholehearted following of Jesus. I know they searched the Scriptures and pursued a deep understanding of the truth. Many believers have pursued the truth and come to similar conclusions. However, on this point, I must say the logic does not make sense. It redefines the story to be *not* what Paul says numerous times in Scripture.

It is not just that, through Christ's death, sin's power has been broken. As Paul says, and as we saw in the last chapter, we are now dead to it. We no longer have sin living in us—not even a little bit. We experience growth and there is struggle, yes, but we are not struggling against a sinful nature anymore.

But what about hyperbole? you may wonder. It is true that Paul was at one point a Jewish teacher and that Jewish teachers often used hyperbole as a teaching technique. Could he have been using exaggerated language about our being dead to sin to make a point?

The problem with this idea is that if Paul was speaking in hyperbole, he chose a profoundly poor time to do so. If this is hyperbole, much of Paul's other salvation logic is undermined and we are left with almost no Gospel.

Here is the conundrum: Paul is saying we are dead to sin because we died with Jesus. He links our death to sin with the death of Jesus. This, however, is not the only thing Paul links to the death of Jesus. Specifically, Jesus' death accomplished three major things for us:

- **Death to sin:** We died along with Jesus on the cross, killing the sin nature that had taken up residence within humanity (see Romans 6:2–4).
- **Death to the Law:** Through the death of Jesus on the cross, we were also freed from the covenant of the Law and its requirements, so our relationship with God is no longer dictated by the Old Covenant (see Romans 7:4).
- **Forgiveness of sins:** Jesus offered Himself on the cross as the sacrifice to pay for sins, rendering all our sins forgiven in His death (see Hebrews 10:12–14).

Each of these hangs on one element: the death of Jesus. It is the death of Jesus that results in the killing of the sinful nature inside of us. It is the death of Jesus that frees us from a performance relationship with God. It is the death of Jesus that stands as the single sacrifice for our sins. Contending that we still have a sinful nature means selectively breaking this argument of what Christ's death did. If I was one with Him as He died on the cross (see Galatians 2:20) but my sinful nature is not dead, then Jesus did not fully die on the cross. If I say Paul is speaking hyperbolically and I am not, in fact, fully dead to sin, what I am really saying is Jesus did not fully die.

That, in itself, is enough for me to throw out the idea of "battling natures." However, it gets worse.

If Jesus did not fully die on the cross, then I am not fully dead to the Law, either, and Jesus did not fully forgive my sins. This means I still have to obey the Law to keep my relationship with God in a good place. It also means my salvation is now by my works and I have to somehow obtain forgiveness for myself. This puts me in the position of saving myself, rather than trusting Jesus to save me.

As you can see, the whole Gospel falls apart. This is because it all hangs together as one piece. Either all these things are accomplished for us in Jesus' death or they all are not. To say Paul is stretching his language in one aspect is to undermine them all.

Indeed, our sinful nature has been killed—and by that, I mean it is dead. Departed. Gone. Cut away from us fully. Set as far from us as the east is from the west. As believers, we need to "get over our bad self," for that self has left, and we are not waiting for him or her to return.

A Question of Struggle

Given that we are not going to keep going down the road of believing dual natures live within us, the natural question is this: What is happening, then? If we are dead to sin completely, what is going on in us? Why do we feel so *not* dead to sin, and what can we do about it? These questions lead us to some practical answers.

The first element we need to understand is this: It is possible, through our own misunderstanding, to undermine the grace God is extending to us in the Gospel. Just like the Israelites in the wilderness, we can miss God's grace if we hear it but do not respond in faith:

For good news came to us just as to them, but the message they heard did not benefit them, because they were not united by faith with those who listened.

Hebrews 4:2

This is a crazy thought! Essentially, the truth can be staring us in the face, but if it is not met with faith, its power will not be activated in our lives. The answer could be right in front of us but be rendered powerless because our faith is aimed in the wrong direction.

Many of us put ourselves in a similar position when we see ourselves as wrestling against a sinful nature. We have faith wrapped around an idea and a perspective—that we are in a battle against ourselves—but this is not how God sees it. God sees you as dead to sin. When we position ourselves as if we are *not* dead to sin and ask for His grace to come to us, we are planting our starting point outside truth. This, in turn, makes it harder for us to receive into our lives what God is doing. We are disagreeing with Him before He even has the chance to get to work!

The Holy Spirit is not going to empower us to fight our sin nature because Jesus has already killed it, and the Spirit is not going to empower us to undermine what Jesus has done. He wants to convict us of our righteousness, not empower us to shadowbox a sin nature that has already been dealt with.

If we reposition ourselves in alignment with His truth and ask for His empowering, God is more than ready to step in and assist. As Hebrews 4:16 says, we can boldly come before His throne of grace and we will find help in our time of need.

So, the first reason we may struggle to live the Christian life is that we try to do it on our own. We disagree with God about what Christ has done and exclude His empowering of us before we even ask for it.

But there is a second reason we struggle: We have an enemy. Even when we start from a point of faith and see ourselves the same way God does, experiencing His grace flowing to us and empowering us to live the way He designed, Satan is still a real player on the field, and he actively resists us. Paul tells us:

> For we do not wrestle against flesh and blood, but against the rulers, against the authorities, against the cosmic powers over this present darkness, against the spiritual forces of evil in the heavenly places.
>
> Ephesians 6:12

Notice Paul's language here: We *do not* wrestle against flesh and blood.[1] Our battle is not on the natural plane; it is on the spiritual plane. We are wrestling with the spiritual forces of evil. That is the struggle we should expect in our lives—a struggle against the enemy, not against ourselves. Many of us see ourselves as wrestling with our own flesh and blood, which is something Paul does not teach, and we do not even consider Satan's role. Yet there is a real battle happening between the Kingdom of heaven and the kingdom of darkness. We are in a fight against Satan and his attempt to rule the earth.

Satan uses two tactics against believers. Either he tries to get too much attention, or he tries to avoid attention altogether. Getting hooked into either of these tactics is not wise. We do not need to glorify the devil, turning him into an exalted foe. He does not deserve that. At the same time, one of the first rules of engagement in combat is never to underestimate your enemy, even if you have strategic advantages.

Satan and his minions are real, and we, as believers, are soldiers in the opposite kingdom. This means we are at the top of their priority list. We should expect to experience pushback everywhere they think they can influence us—and one of their most fruitful tactics is to camouflage themselves and to suggest to us that we are struggling with some part of ourselves when, in reality, we are experiencing their siege tactics.

A Question of Growth

The previous two struggles we discussed are external ones. We can struggle because we lack the grace and empowerment of the Spirit, and we can struggle because we have a real enemy who is trying to subdue us. But additionally, we can struggle through the process of our own internal growth. However, that growth is not a struggle against our flesh. It is actually something quite different. And examining how it works leads us to an understanding of how we can better cooperate with God in our journey toward maturity in our faith.

The reason we interpret our current struggles as wrestling with a not-fully-dead sin nature is because somewhere in the back of our minds, we have a faulty model for how the different aspects of our humanity—our nature, our desires and our actions—fit together. Namely, we know that our desires spring from somewhere, and we believe they come from our nature, which is the deepest core of who we are. What we are inclined toward flows from our being, we think, and those desires tend to play themselves out in our actions. Since our desires are sometimes sinful, we conclude that our nature is partially sinful, too. Such a belief model might look like this:

Nature	influences	**Desires**	influences	**Actions**
Partially alive to sin		Drawn to sin at times		Sinful actions

This is the picture we project onto Scripture. When we read passages like Romans 8 or Galatians 5, where Paul talks about walking according to the Spirit and not the flesh, we see ourselves in a struggle with our flesh—the unredeemed part of ourselves that is poking its head out through our sinful inclinations. It feels like it fits, so we internalize this picture. But even though it seems to describe our experience, it does not sit well with the logic of Scripture. In this picture, we use Romans 8 to undermine what Paul says in Romans 6—that we are dead to sin—and Galatians 5 to invalidate Galatians 2, where Paul says that although we were dead in our sins, now we are alive in Christ.

What if the problem is that the model above is too simple? What if there is another option? In fact, we know it is too simple. Just because we have a desire to sin at any given moment, we know that does not guarantee we *will* sin. God has given us a will, and we can use our will to resist temptation. In that scenario, we find another element interfering with and overriding our desire:

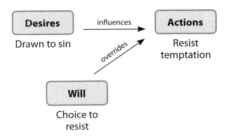

However, even this model has its shortcomings. If this is the way you see and experience yourself, then your journey to Christian maturity is going to be one of primarily exercising the will. You are still stuck with a partially sinful nature, so the road toward being more Christlike is one of getting better and better at using your will to check your nature when necessary. The focus is on managing behavior. Unfortunately, as discussed earlier, you do this without God's empowering grace because you are trying to fight a battle God has not called you to fight. No wonder it feels exhausting and like you will never get ahead!

What if there is a missing piece from both of these pictures? And what if that missing piece is something that could modify our desires? If such a piece exists, it would be possible for us to be fully righteous—100 percent dead to sin—but still have sinful desires.

Believe it or not, a crystal-clear example of this exists in Scripture. We find it way back at the beginning:

> So when the woman saw that the tree was good for food, and that it was a delight to the eyes, and that the tree *was to be desired* to make one wise, she took of its fruit and ate, and she also gave some to her husband who was with her, and he ate.
>
> Genesis 3:6, emphasis mine

When Eve sinned by eating the fruit of the Tree of Knowledge of Good and Evil, she desired it before she ate it. Here was Eve, the co-pinnacle of creation, made in the image of God. She had no sin nature. Sin had never happened in human history. Yet here she was, desiring something forbidden.

What happened to bring about that desire? Eve did not desire the fruit at all before she started having a conversation with the serpent. But as she listened to the serpent, *her perspective of the truth changed.* That perspective shift changed her desire, even though she did not have a sinful nature.

This means our desires are not simply a reflection of our nature. They are influenced by our nature, yes, but also by the way we see the world. The way we see the world—what we assume to be true about it—might be called our *mindset.*

It was Eve's mindset that changed when she talked with Satan. Before that conversation, she had implicit trust in God and did not see any reason to head in a direction other than where He led. But after the conversation, she believed there was some benefit to choosing differently. That belief, or mindset, changed her desire.

Now, here is the kicker. When we are saved, we are made new. Our nature is changed. We become 100 percent dead to sin, just like Eve was. But our mind is not completely regenerated at the moment of salvation. We still live with a mindset formed by our life experiences and various influences. While God gives us a new heart and a new spirit, our mind is still in the process of being renewed. Remember what Paul says:

> Do not be conformed to this world, but be transformed by the renewal of your mind, that by testing you may discern what is the will of God, what is good and acceptable and perfect.
>
> Romans 12:2

How are we not conformed to this world—by warring against a sinful nature? No. By renewing our mind! This is what transforms us.[2]

We are not split with a righteous part and a sinful part. We are righteous, period—but we are learning how to live that out. Our journey is one of discovering what it means to be a new creation and how to live in alignment with that truth. A more complete picture of what is happening inside of each of us is this:

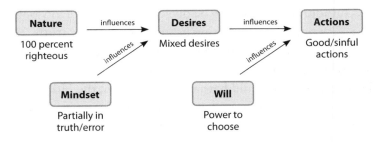

From this drawing, we can see that when our mindset is aligned with our righteous nature, we can expect to experience godly desires. The fruit of these godly desires will be godly actions. This is the way God designed us to live. This is what the Christian walk is meant to look like.

Paul ties all of this together and explains this process in Ephesians 4 (with my clarifying notes in brackets):

> They [unbelievers] have become callous and have given themselves up to sensuality, greedy to practice every kind of impurity. [Note the context here: sinful actions.] But that is not the way you learned Christ!—assuming that you have heard about him and were taught in him, as the truth is in Jesus, to put off your old self [putting off the old self means not "wearing" an old self of sinful actions over the new self underneath; the word he chooses here is the word for taking off a coat], which belongs to your former manner of life and is corrupt through deceitful desires [our desires leading to sin are deceitful—they are based on a deception in our mindset], and to be renewed in the spirit of your minds [these desires are dealt with by allowing the Spirit to renew our minds and to bring us out of a mindset of deception into truth], and to put on the new self, created after the likeness of God in true righteousness and holiness [this allows us to "wear" the new self, instead of the old self, resulting in the likeness of God in true righteousness and holiness, as revealed in our outer actions].
>
> Ephesians 4:19–24

Our journey is meant to be one of allowing the Holy Spirit to renew our minds and bring us into a mindset of truth. The problem is that we are spending time and energy battling "ourselves," which renders us stagnant and unproductive, since that is not what God would have us do. In reality, the Holy Spirit is trying to speak to us and grow us up. But we are focused on ourselves instead of what God is saying.

It is a sad reality that many of us spend more time shadow-boxing an old, dead nature than hearing the living God as He is working to grow us up in Christ. Paul described the correct pursuit we ought to have in Philippians 3:

> Not that I have already obtained this or am already perfect, but I press on to make it my own, because Christ Jesus has made me his own. Brothers, I do not consider that I have made it my own. But one thing I do: *forgetting* what lies behind and straining forward to what lies ahead, I press on toward the goal for the prize of the upward call of God in Christ Jesus. Let those of us who are mature *think* this way, and if in anything you think otherwise, God will reveal that also to you. *Only let us hold true to what we have attained.*
>
> Philippians 3:12–16, emphasis mine

Paul saw himself growing into the ability to be true to what had already been given him. God had already made him a new creation. To live that out, he made a pursuit of forgetting the way he used to see things in order to grow into a new way of thinking, which he says God reveals as we need it.

A Question of Renewal

The next natural question is this: How, then, do we renew our mind? Are we supposed to spend every moment of every day monitoring our every thought and trying to correct each one? Should we confess Scripture all day, every day?

It is a good idea to pay attention to your thoughts and to confess Scripture, but the basic fact of the matter is that you cannot renew your own mind. The Spirit has to do it. You cannot bring yourself into truth. The Spirit is here to do that for you:

For who knows a person's thoughts except the spirit of that person, which is in him? So also no one comprehends the thoughts of God except the Spirit of God. Now we have received not the spirit of the world, but the Spirit who is from God, that we might understand the things freely given us by God.

1 Corinthians 2:11–12

Did you catch what Paul said here? He said we have the Holy Spirit and that the Holy Spirit knows God's thoughts. The Holy Spirit knows God's mindset, and He teaches us to think the way God thinks. Why? So we may comprehend the things God has already given us.

The Holy Spirit is here to unpack our understanding of the new creation God has made us to be. It is a reality that has already occurred, but we do not understand everything it means, nor do we know how to live it out. The Spirit knows all these things, and He loves to change the way we see. He loves to take the things of the Father and the Son and make them known to us. He is the Spirit of truth, who is here to guide us into *all* truth.

We cannot grow ourselves as believers. We can only learn to cooperate with the Spirit to allow Him to grow us. We can get in the way and shut down what God is doing, but we cannot pull ourselves up by our own bootstraps.

As a result of all this, our heart posture is critical. Are we prayerfully in submission and openness, expecting the Spirit of God to guide us into truth more and more every day? Are we willing to let God edit what we think is true about the world?

I have discovered that I do not always know what truth I am living. Much of my life is the result of thoughts I do not remember having or choices I do not remember making many years ago. Experiences have shaped me far more than I see and in ways I do not understand. I do not even know where I need to experience my mind being renewed.

As a result, I want to take the posture that God is free to adjust anything in me. I want to give God an open canvas with my life and allow Him to choose what to do. Whenever I notice thoughts or emotions surfacing—usually through experiences I know we are supposed to live above, such as fear, hurt, anger or otherwise—I ask the Spirit to speak to me and adjust my thinking. I am okay if He does not tell me what He is doing, as long as He is doing it. I do not have to understand what is happening in order for God to change me. I just want to be more and more aligned with Him.

Again, it is not something we can create or coerce to happen. It is the by-product of our relationship with the Spirit, which we invest in. At any given time, we are either in sync or out of sync with that relationship. Either we have our heart inclined toward the Spirit, with an open ear to Him, or we are distracted and preoccupied with our own life.

This is the dynamic Paul is referencing in Romans 8, where he says:

> For those who live according to the flesh set their minds on the things of the flesh, but those who live according to the Spirit set their minds on the things of the Spirit. For to set the mind on the flesh is death, but to set the mind on the Spirit is life and peace.
>
> Romans 8:5–6

These are Paul's instructions for living out the reality he described in Romans 6, where he says:

> We were buried therefore with him by baptism into death, in order that, just as Christ was raised from the dead by the glory of the Father, we too might walk in newness of life.
>
> Romans 6:4

Paul is saying that if we want to live "plugged in" to the natural world—the flesh—that lifestyle is supported by a focus on the flesh. When our predominant attention is given to the things on this natural plane, like our concerns, worries, problems, relationships, finances, health and even our sin habits, we have our mind set here. And because this world is fallen, to focus here is to further entrench the problem. It is to further cement the world's perspective in our mindset, which results in "death," or the manifestation of the brokenness in our mindset.

If, however, we want to live connected to the Spirit, allowing Him to be the predominant factor in the way we live our lives, we need to direct our attention to the realities of the spirit realm—namely, who we are in Christ, what God has done for us, God's redemptive plan for this world, and the attributes of His heart toward us and the world. As we fixate on those realities, keeping the posture of our heart open to the direction and leading of the Spirit, we provide plenty of space for the life and peace of God to flow into us. We live with a mindset in alignment with our righteous nature.

I want you to see that Paul continually instructs us to live in this kind of moment-by-moment relationship with the Holy Spirit, walking relationally with Him and allowing Him to empower who Christ has made us to be. He does it even beyond the pages of Romans. Let's take a look at what he says in Galatians 5 (again with my clarifying notes in brackets):

> But I say, walk by the Spirit, and you will not gratify the desires of the flesh. [If we walk relationally with the Spirit, we will not live out the desires of the world.] For the desires of the flesh are against the Spirit, and the desires of the Spirit are against the flesh, for these are opposed to each other, to keep you from doing the things you want to do. [The desires the world creates in you

are the opposite of the desires the Spirit creates in you.] But if you are led by the Spirit, you are not under the law. [You do not need to worry about monitoring your behavior if you are in step with the Spirit, as what will come out will be good, not sin.] Now the works of the flesh are evident: sexual immorality, impurity, sensuality, idolatry, sorcery, enmity, strife, jealousy, fits of anger, rivalries, dissensions, divisions, envy, drunkenness, orgies, and things like these. I warn you, as I warned you before, that those who do such things will not inherit the kingdom of God. [This is what the world without God looks like. If the world becomes our focus, this is the life we will live out. Sinful actions hinder the releasing of the rule of God through our lives.] But the fruit of the Spirit is love, joy, peace, patience, kindness, goodness, faithfulness, gentleness, self-control; against such things there is no law. [These are the qualities the Spirit cultivates in you as you relationally walk with Him.] And those who belong to Christ Jesus have crucified the flesh with its passions and desires. [You have already died to the natural world and are now alive because the Spirit has born you again in Christ.]

If we live by the Spirit, let us also keep in step with the Spirit. [Since the Spirit is the reason you're alive, live in step with Him now.]

Galatians 5:16–25

Here, Paul is not at all discussing an inner conflict of us warring against "our flesh." In fact, he never indicates ownership of the flesh at all; he always uses the term "*the* flesh." When did "the flesh" become "our flesh"? At some point, we internalized the process he describes for living out our righteous nature. We turned it into an inner conflict that reinforces what he warns us against. By focusing on a duel between two natures, our focus remains on the flesh. When we focus on the sins we are still committing and the fallen nature we are still allegedly wrestling with, we shove out of focus what Christ has done and do not live in submission to the Spirit's empowerment. Therefore, we reap the exact things Paul warns will creep into our lives.

This mindset is pervasive in and dangerous to the body of Christ. We mean well, but we undermine our ability to live inside the grace God provides. I have seen the fruit of this thinking bear out in many lives. But as we move into alignment with God's truth about who we are, we are empowered and freed to live as He calls us to live.

Clay Harrington is a pastor at our church whom God is using to bring scores into the Kingdom of God. His journey has been one of learning to leave behind a false picture of himself and embrace who God says he is. Here is how he describes his journey:

> "I'm just a sinner saved by grace . . ."
>
> This was a phrase I heard a lot throughout my life, and even more so when I decided to live for Jesus. For me, this phrase unconsciously helped me form an understanding that I was a sinner, even after giving my life to Christ.
>
> When I identified with being a sinner rather than a saint, I would constantly struggle with sin. I read books about the doctrine of "indwelling sin," and passages such as Romans 7 and Jeremiah 17:9 would further solidify my understanding of my struggle with sin and how it's impossible to live free from it.
>
> One day, I remember reading Romans 6:11 as though I was reading it for the first time. I had read the whole Bible at least three or four times by then, but this time was different. This time I felt as if Jesus was saying to me, "Clay, you're DEAD to sin!" This was a startling revelation!
>
> As I pressed into what I felt Jesus telling me, I began to study the letters of Paul from this new lens and found myself continually amazed. Teachings from Graham Cooke, Dan Mohler and even my bro Putty Putman, as I went through the School of Kingdom Ministry, would help solidify the truth that I am a new creation who isn't mastered by sin any longer.

This new revelation, Scripture study and teachings on be
dead to sin all coalesced to bear remarkable fruit in my lifi
found a new power to actually deny the impulse to lust after
women and the urge to gamble. Fits of rage that had a strong-
hold on me for years seemed to lose their grip. No longer did
offense, gossip or pride consume me, because I had embraced a
new identity. Instead of believing the phrase "I'm a sinner saved
by grace . . . ," I now believe that I *was* a sinner who *was* saved
by grace; now I'm a saint!

Paul passionately advises, "If we are indeed in Christ . . .
then we must consider ourselves dead to sin and alive to God."
Now that I don't consider myself mastered by sin, I've found
I'm able to live in a new level of freedom from it.

A Question of Letting Go

I was raised to carry the picture I described earlier in this chapter.
I saw myself as wrestling with a sin nature, and this description
seemed to describe my experience. Then, as God began to give
me a new picture, I found it difficult to let go of my old one.
Looking back, I am surprised how strongly I was attached to
that previous picture of myself! Somehow, I wanted to believe
there was something in me that still needed to be killed.

We may struggle to change our perspective on this because
it increases the level of responsibility we have to take for our
lives. We find ourselves no longer wrestling with something that
renders us powerless, like our sin nature. Instead, we start struggling with our mindset or deceptions—and this means there
is no excuse for our misbehavior. We cannot pass the buck on
to a sin nature. We are responsible for what we choose to do.
Even if we struggle with sinful desires, it is our responsibility
to bring them before God and allow the Spirit to minister His
truth and freedom to us. We are now meant to partner with
God to form every bit of our life experience, both inward and
outward.

The previous way of living internalizes our failures into an identity ("I am still a sinner"), and this is profoundly shaming and detrimental to living a life that looks like Jesus. Believing we are still broken limits the way we see ourselves. We do not see ourselves the same way God sees us because we disagree with His starting point. Thus, it is difficult for us to accept God's love because we cannot fully love ourselves. There are parts of ourselves we love and other parts we hate. We wonder, How could God feel any different toward us?

The result is that we do not live a life that looks like the one to which Scripture calls us. We are a house divided against ourselves, and we experience exactly what Jesus said: We cannot stand. Our walk with Christ becomes frustrating and disappointing. Sin plays as big a part in our experience as our relationship with God does.

It has been a long journey for me to learn how to let go of the image of "dueling Puttys"—years, to be honest. I do not think it needs to take that long for everyone, but I was fearful I might be turning into a heretic as the Lord began to reveal this truth to me through Scripture.

Is it possible I have gotten this teaching wrong? Absolutely. I must concede that. I am a human being, after all. I do not have perfect knowledge any more than anyone else does.

However, the way we know the quality of a message is by the quality of its fruit. When people ask me why they should take this idea I am presenting seriously, especially since it is not the "orthodox view," I turn to Jesus. Jesus makes it clear that fruit is the standard by which we must measure these things:

> "Beware of false prophets, who come to you in sheep's clothing but inwardly are ravenous wolves. You will recognize them by their fruits. Are grapes gathered from thornbushes, or figs from thistles? So, every healthy tree bears good fruit, but the

diseased tree bears bad fruit. A healthy tree cannot bear bad fruit, nor can a diseased tree bear good fruit. Every tree that does not bear good fruit is cut down and thrown into the fire. Thus you will recognize them by their fruits."

Matthew 7:15–20

When it comes to the fruit of living by this teaching, it turns out the fruit in my own life—and the fruit I have seen multiplied in others' lives—has been exactly the kind of fruit Jesus talks about. It is the same fruit Paul talks about in Galatians 5, too.

I have felt a profound change in my faith. I feel closer to God, and my relationship with Him has profoundly grown. I love others more effectively. I am a better husband and parent. I wrestle less with temptation, and it is easier to overcome it. Even though growth is uncomfortable, when I hit a growth point in my Christian walk, it is more of a joyful partnership with the Holy Spirit than a painful struggle. The Gospel continues to become more and more significant to me. It has transformed the lens through which I see myself and the rest of the world.

I love my journey with Jesus. It is the best part of my life. And I want this same journey for you. I urge you to leave behind the picture of yourself as "mostly dead" to sin and to pick up a new mentality—one I am convinced is more biblical—that says you are now completely dead to sin and learning how to be a new creation.

THINKING LIKE JESUS

- Believers are fully dead to their sin nature. We do not wrestle with our flesh or continue to deal with our sin nature.

- Our journey is now one of having our mind renewed so that every part of us aligns with the righteousness God has already given us. As that happens, our desires are directed toward the things of the Lord and we naturally live out our new creation nature.

- The Holy Spirit is the One who knows how to renew our mind. He renews our mind as we walk in relationship with Him.

7

What about Forgiveness?

In the last few chapters, we have focused on the topic of our nature. We have asked, What does it mean to be dead to sin and alive to God? Now that we have clarity around how that works, let's revisit forgiveness. How does forgiveness fit into the picture we have been developing so far?

It is helpful to start with where the forgiveness of sins entered the biblical story. We know the need for regeneration was introduced in the Garden of Eden. Did the need for forgiveness of sins begin there, too?

To address this question, we first need to define what we mean by *forgiveness*. In our relationships, we almost constantly forgive one another of little misunderstandings. A friend or spouse says something that comes across not how they meant it, and we choose to see it as a misunderstanding and move on, based upon trust. But while this is an expression of forgiveness, it is not usually what we mean when we talk about forgiveness from a theological point of view. When it comes to forgiveness as a salvation mechanism, we usually mean the restoration of a broken-down relationship.

At what point, then, did our sinful actions break our relationship with God in such a way that we had to deal with those actions in order to restore the relationship?

This is an important question. We may assume forgiveness was required as soon as Adam and Eve committed sinful actions at the Fall. Their sinful actions did require forgiveness in the context of their relationship with God, but there is a difference between that and the relationship breaking down completely because of their sinful actions.

In fact, forgiveness as a relational breakdown did not occur until much later in the story. Consider a few of the examples we see in the book of Genesis:

- When Adam and Eve sinned and had their ensuing conversation with God, there were consequences to their actions, but God took the initiative to care for them. He clothed them, and there was no discussion of forgiveness. (See Genesis 3:8–24.)
- When Cain killed Abel and was cursed—by the ground, not by God—God stepped in to protect him after he expressed his fear of being unable to bear the consequences of his actions. (See Genesis 4:9–15.)
- When Abraham lied—twice—about Sarah being his sister instead of his wife, God covered for him, protecting him from the consequences of his bad choices and bringing them through unscathed. (See Genesis 12:10–20; 20:1–18.)

In fact, throughout the book of Genesis, there is no discussion of the need for forgiveness. We see a whole lot of people making really bad choices, but those choices do not seem to break their relationship with God. If anything, God gets *more* involved at times, in order to help people with the consequences of their bad choices.

Rather than relational breakdown, a better description of what happened between God and mankind at the Fall is *distance*. Man forgot who God was and what He was like. Trust broke down. Therefore, God began looking for people who had faith—trust in who He was—and began to work with them.

Noah and Abraham are the early examples of people who trusted God and whose trust allowed them to move past estrangement into relationship. In the stories of these two men, we see a great deal of discussion about righteousness, but no discussion of forgiveness. Noah is portrayed as righteous (see Genesis 6:9). Abraham bargains with God about the number of righteous people in Sodom and Gomorrah (see Genesis 18:22–33). Righteousness exists independent of the idea of a "clean slate before God," because the world was still broken by sin. Rather, it refers to parts of creation that were not twisted away from the original design by the working of sin.[1]

When Offense Entered In

If, after the Garden of Eden, we experienced estrangement from God, at what point did sin become a barrier that broke down our relationship with God? When did sin become a wall that kept us out of relationship with God? At what point did the offense become so real that it needed to be dealt with?

This question is answered when the Israelites are given the Law at Mount Sinai. The Law changed the dynamic of the way God and the Israelites related from that point forward.

When Moses brought the Israelites to Mount Sinai, a tragic event happened. It started with God declaring to the Israelite people His intentions for them as a nation. He began by giving Moses a message for the Israelites:

"'You yourselves have seen what I did to the Egyptians, and how I bore you on eagles' wings and brought you to myself. Now therefore, if you will indeed obey my voice and keep my covenant, you shall be my treasured possession among all peoples, for all the earth is mine; and you shall be to me a kingdom of priests and a holy nation.' These are the words that you shall speak to the people of Israel."

Exodus 19:4–6

God desired the entire nation to have direct access to Him and to be a nation of priests to the rest of the world. Every Israelite was to act as a priest to all the other people groups in the world.

The Israelites agreed to God's purpose, and God indicated He would come down to prove Moses was telling the truth:

So Moses came and called the elders of the people and set before them all these words that the LORD had commanded him. All the people answered together and said, "All that the LORD has spoken we will do." And Moses reported the words of the people to the LORD. And the LORD said to Moses, "Behold, I am coming to you in a thick cloud, that the people may hear when I speak with you, and may also believe you forever."

Exodus 19:7–9

God did come down onto the mountain, and it was intense! Thunder and lightning whipped around the mountain, and fire and smoke billowed up like a volcano. In fear of the power of God's presence, the Israelites changed their mind and asked for Moses to interact with God on their behalf so they did not have to:

Now when all the people saw the thunder and the flashes of lightning and the sound of the trumpet and the mountain smoking, the people were afraid and trembled, and they stood far off and said to Moses, "You speak to us, and we will listen; but do not let God speak to us, lest we die."

Exodus 20:18–19

Moses tried to shift the situation, but he was unsuccessful:

Moses said to the people, "Do not fear, for God has come to test you, that the fear of him may be before you, that you may not sin." The people stood far off, while Moses drew near to the thick darkness where God was.

Exodus 20:20–21

The Israelites asked for a different relationship from what God intended. They basically told Moses, "We don't want to be priests. We want *you* to be the priest. We don't want direct access to God. We want something between God and us to protect us, because He's scary!"

The relationship God intended was not the relationship the Israelites got. Rather than being a kingdom of priests to the rest of the world, a tribe of priests (the Levites) were given to the rest of Israel. The people's request for an indirect relationship with God resulted in a covenant—the Law—designed to keep distance between God and them.

The Law was not God's intention. It was His compromise with the Israelites, who did not want direct access to Him.

The Law also introduced another new dynamic. It introduced the idea of being on God's "good list" or "bad list." In other words, the covenant of the Law created categories that affected the way God related to humanity. This is what Paul meant when he made statements like this:

For sin indeed was in the world before the law was given, but sin is not counted where there is no law.

Romans 5:13

Sin existed since the Fall, but the Law introduced a way to "keep score" of sin. It was only at this point that the concept of needing to deal with sin debt in order to restore relationship with God began to make sense. What we usually think of as forgiveness is the act of God moving us from the bad list to the good list under the covenant of the Law. This is why there are explicit instructions throughout the book of Leviticus about how to appropriate forgiveness in various situations. The priests began to step into a new role, one of helping people manage their relationship with God within the context of the covenant of the Law.

Most of us believe the requirement of forgiveness for the restitution of sin is universally true—that it is built into the nature of God or the universe. I do not believe that is an accurate picture. Instead, it is an element of the covenant of the Law. Outside the context of the Law, sin and consequences of sin exist, but those consequences do not include the cut-off from God that happens when we sin under the Law.

If we closely read the story of the Israelites and their covenants with God, we see this picture depicted. In Leviticus 26 and Deuteronomy 28, we find extensive lists describing the blessings available to the people when they followed the Law, and the curses and ways God would come against the people if they turned away from the Law. This is Scripture describing exactly how "sin breaks our relationship with God" works in the Law.

The consequences of violating the commandments of the Law resulted in a position of God being against us. This is what Scripture refers to as "wrath":

> For the *law* brings wrath, but where there is no law there is no transgression.
>
> Romans 4:15, emphasis mine

This is remarkable. It tells us wrath is not a property of God's nature; it is a property of the Law. It is the covenant of the Law that puts God in a position of judgment against us when we sin. God has no affinity for sin, but it is only in the context of the Law that God is duty bound to *punish* and pour judgment down upon it.

The effects of this arrangement bear out in the book of Exodus. For the entirety of their journey from the Red Sea to Mount Sinai, the Israelites grumbled and complained about God's provision for them. The water was not good enough. The food was unsatisfying. All the while, God put up with them and provided for them. But as soon as the Law was given, any infraction was quickly and harshly addressed, and usually involved death.

Did God's attitude change? No. The rules of relationship changed, because the Israelites demanded a covenant of performance rather than one of connection and relationship.

The book of Hebrews reveals to us God's heart concerning this arrangement:

> For if that first covenant had been faultless, there would have been no occasion to look for a second. For he finds fault with [the promises of the Law] when he says: "Behold, the days are coming, declares the Lord, when I will establish a new covenant with the house of Israel and with the house of Judah, not like the covenant that I made with their fathers on the day when I took them by the hand to bring them out of the land of Egypt. *For they did not continue in my covenant, and so I showed no concern for them*, declares the Lord.
>
> Hebrews 8:7–9, emphasis mine

God states here that He did not like the arrangement of the Law because He had to treat the Israelites poorly when they were on the bad list. He did not like having to curse His people because they were not able to keep the covenant.

This is why Jesus came and instituted a New Covenant. It was in order to remove this dynamic.

When Sacrifice Became Necessary

When the Law was introduced, it introduced another salvation need. Every person was born a sinner and in need of redemption, but those born under the Law had to deal with the judgment of the Law:

> For all who have sinned without the law will also perish without the law, and all who have sinned under the law will be judged by the law.
>
> Romans 2:12

This means that a person under the Law needed to be made new, but also needed to be forgiven:

	Outside the Law	Under the Law
Salvation needs	Redemption	Redemption Forgiveness

We now have two problems that need to be solved, and the Gospel solves them differently because they have different sources. First, we need to be redeemed because sin has come to dwell within us; this problem is located within our being. Second, we need to be forgiven because the Law demanded wrath where it had been trespassed.

We have already looked at how we are made new. By faith, we are joined with Jesus in His death and resurrection. Forgiveness, however, works differently because it is connected to a relationship detailed by a covenant. Just as that covenant determined the conditions of transgression, it also determined the conditions required for forgiveness. The condition required for forgiveness was sacrifice and shedding of blood:

> Indeed, under the law almost everything is purified with blood, and without the shedding of blood there is no forgiveness of sins.
>
> Hebrews 9:22

Under the Law, sacrifice, according to the covenant, brought forgiveness. Faith was not involved in the equation. As Paul says, "The law is not of faith" (Galatians 3:12). Faith does interact with the story of forgiveness, as we will soon see, but it happens a little differently than we may expect.

The book of Hebrews makes clear that Jesus offered Himself as the Lamb of God—the single sacrifice to fulfill the requirement of forgiveness for everyone for all time:

> And every priest stands daily at his service, offering repeatedly the same sacrifices, which can never take away sins. But when Christ had offered for all time a single sacrifice for sins, he sat down at the right hand of God, waiting from that time until his enemies should be made a footstool for his feet.
>
> Hebrews 10:11–13

Jesus was the sin sacrifice required by the Law for everyone, and therefore everyone has been forgiven. God has closed the gap and extended His forgiveness to all through the work of His Son. This is what Paul refers to in 2 Corinthians (with my clarifying notes in brackets):

> Therefore, if anyone is in Christ, he is a new creation. The old has passed away; behold, the new has come. [We are made new when we are joined to Christ by faith.] All this is from God, who through Christ reconciled us to himself and gave us the ministry

of reconciliation [we are not only reconciled to God, but we are sent to reconcile others to God]; that is, in Christ God was reconciling the world to himself, not counting their trespasses against them, and entrusting to us the message of reconciliation [in Jesus, God closed the chasm the trespasses of the whole world created; they are not being counted against anyone anymore]. Therefore, we are ambassadors for Christ, God making his appeal through us. We implore you on behalf of Christ, be reconciled to God. [God sends us to tell others that because He has closed the gap on His side by forgiving us, the appropriate response is to receive that forgiveness and come into relationship with Him.] For our sake he made him to be sin who knew no sin, so that in him we might become the righteousness of God. [The purpose of all of this is to enter into the righteousness that God is offering us in Christ. When we are restored to relationship, He makes us new.]

2 Corinthians 5:17–21

Paul is saying that everyone has been forgiven. God has reconciled the whole world to Himself. The problem is not that any specific person has not been forgiven. The problem is that they have not *received* that forgiveness and come back into relationship with God.

This is where the role of faith enters in. God has issued forgiveness, but it requires faith on our side to receive that forgiveness. God has closed the gap. He has welcomed everyone home. When we trust Him and accept that welcome, we receive and begin to walk in the forgiveness that has been extended to us.

Let me clarify with an example. Let's say I borrowed something important to you and I lost it—something irreplaceable, maybe a family heirloom. There is a good chance that would introduce a breakdown in our relationship. I would have sinned against you, and it would result in the need for reconciliation between us. Since the object was irreplaceable, I could not fix the problem by buying you a new one. Therefore, our relationship would be stuck, unreconciled.

This is akin to our situation with God and our debt under the Law. Something negative was introduced into the relationship, and we did not have the capacity to reconcile because of it.

Now, in this scenario I have posed, what would happen if I saw you at church or bumped into you in the supermarket? I would feel guilty. I would know you were angry with me, so I would try to avoid you. If I could not avoid you, I would try to keep the conversation short and exit as soon as possible, because I would know there was nothing I could do to mend our relationship. I would be guilty before you.

Suppose one day, you decided to forgive me. In your heart, you released me from the debt I owed you and decided to be open to rebuilding our relationship. You would have reconciled yourself to me. You would have removed the obstacle to our relationship, and I would have been forgiven.

This does not mean our relationship would be rebuilt. The next time I saw you, I would still try to avoid you. I would still feel guilty and ashamed. Even though you had forgiven me, I had not received it. I would not know I was forgiven, so I would not be reconciled to you. In my eyes, I would still be guilty and the relationship would still be impossible. I would be forgiven, but I would not be living in the reality of that. I would be living inside the perception of your unforgiveness.

Let's say you realized I was avoiding you and, despite your best efforts, you could not get through to me that you had forgiven me. I was just too good at dodging you. What would you do? You would probably send a friend to tell me you had forgiven me and that you desire to reconcile our relationship. That friend would tell me how you really feel and invite me to be reconciled to you because you have already reconciled me to yourself. At that point, I would receive your forgiveness. I was forgiven either way, but now I could begin to live in the reality of that forgiveness.

This is how God relates to the world now. He has forgiven the world, thereby removing the obstacle to relationship. He sends us out as His friends to tell the world He desires relationship and to invite them into relationship with Him.

The world is already forgiven! This is a big deal! However, the way we commonly frame the Gospel is unhelpful because we do not impart this truth. We usually convey a message along these lines: "God would like to forgive you, but you have to repent first. When you repent, God will forgive you." The problem with this thinking is that it makes repentance the work we have to do in order to earn forgiveness. Sure, it says God has closed most of the chasm, but our own repentance is what gets us forgiven. This can lead to many questions: Did I repent enough? Was my repentance genuine? Was his or her repentance sincere? All of these questions hang on the idea that our repentance earns our salvation in some way.

What if repentance is not what allows God to forgive us but what allows us to see we have already been forgiven? What if repentance has more to do with turning toward what God says is true and not what we believe is true? What if repentance is how we receive the forgiveness God has already extended to us, not what allows God to forgive us in the first place?

John the Baptist, who epitomized the Law, proclaimed that repentance earned forgiveness:[2]

And he went into all the region around the Jordan, proclaiming a baptism of repentance for the forgiveness of sins.

Luke 3:3

But when Peter preached to the council of priests, he indicated a different relationship between God and man, due to Christ's work on the cross and His resurrection:[3]

"God exalted him at his right hand as Leader and Savior, to give repentance to Israel and forgiveness of sins."

Acts 5:31

Note that Peter does not say repentance *for* the forgiveness of sins but repentance *and* the forgiveness of sins. God has already extended forgiveness, so you get to repent and receive that forgiveness.

This language is consistent throughout the book of Acts. Peter later says:

"To him all the prophets bear witness that everyone who believes in him *receives* forgiveness of sins through his name."

Acts 10:43, emphasis mine

Later still, Paul speaks of Christ's words to him on the road to Damascus and how he was sent to preach

"that they may *receive* forgiveness of sins and a place among those who are sanctified by faith in [Jesus]."

Acts 26:18, emphasis mine

Each time, the language does not say that people would *be* forgiven but that they would *receive* forgiveness. We usually gloss over this because we think being forgiven is the same thing as receiving forgiveness, but indeed they are different, and the language in the New Testament (both before and after the event of the cross) is precise.

Our Gospel is not, "God is ticked off, but if you apologize, He will get over it." That is not great news, honestly, and it does not match the heart of Jesus. Jesus was always forgiving people without them asking for it. When Peter betrayed Jesus, Jesus forgave him and invited him back into relationship without Peter having asked for forgiveness (see John 21). Jesus forgave the Pharisees as He hung on the cross (see Luke 23:34). Jesus was always modeling this reality. He was always walking in complete forgiveness of the sins of the people around Him, constantly inviting them to change their mindset and come into relationship with Him. In fact, I am not aware of any instance where Jesus forgave someone because they asked for it. He preemptively forgave people almost continually.

This is the heart of God. We carry to the world this amazing news: God has already forgiven them. He is a loving God. Why not get to know Him? Why not discover the relationship into which He is inviting you?

When a New Covenant Emerged

Jesus not only grants us the forgiveness we need under the Law through His sacrifice. He also introduces a new covenant and frees us from the old. Paul tells us:

> Likewise, my brothers, you also have died to the law through the body of Christ, so that you may belong to another, to him who has been raised from the dead, in order that we may bear fruit for God. . . . But now we are released from the law, having died to that which held us captive, so that we serve in the new way of the Spirit and not in the old way of the written code.
>
> Romans 7:4, 6

In Jesus, we have died to the Law and been set free from the Old Covenant. We no longer try to live according to the rules and precepts drawn up there, but rather according to the leading of the Spirit of God. Notice, though, that while all have been forgiven, it is only those who are in Christ, by faith, who die to the Law and are freed to enter into the New Covenant.

We find this New Covenant outlined in the book of Hebrews:

"For this is the covenant that I will make with the house of Israel after those days, declares the Lord: I will put my laws into their minds, and write them on their hearts, and I will be their God, and they shall be my people. And they shall not teach, each one his neighbor and each one his brother, saying, 'Know the Lord,' for they shall all know me, from the least of them to the greatest. For I will be merciful toward their iniquities, and I will remember their sins no more."

Hebrews 8:10–12

The promise is that God will come and work on the inside of us, making us new and renewing our minds. The relationship will be one of direct access and knowing God intimately. The arrangement is empowered by the last statements: God has promised to be merciful toward all of our errors and to remember our sins no more. No longer can sin separate us from God. No longer do we need forgiveness to be put back into relationship with God.[4]

Our New Covenant is a covenant of forgiveness and guaranteed relationship. When we sin, we do not break our relationship with God. Instead we sin within the context of that relationship, and God immediately gets to work, extending His grace to us to bring us into the wholeness of a renewed mind so we can look more and more like Jesus. We have the kind of relationship God always intended for us.

Jesus' creation of the New Covenant opened a new kind of relationship with God to us, one where there is family commitment between Him and us. He says we shall all know Him. This is why, after Jesus resurrected, He passed on these instructions to His disciples:

"I am ascending to my Father and your Father, to my God and your God."

John 20:17

Before Jesus instituted the New Covenant, only He called God "Father," because only He had that level of relationship with Him. In the New Covenant, we are all granted direct access to and relationship with God. The desire of the Father that was hijacked by the fear of the Israelites at Mount Sinai has been fulfilled in His Son. Now we can become the priesthood God originally intended them to be, too—which we will discuss in the next chapter.

When Questions Crop Up

Before we conclude this chapter, let me address a few important questions that often crop up.

Question #1: If everyone is forgiven, is everyone saved?

Great question. The answer is no, everyone is most definitely not saved. Salvation does not hinge on forgiveness; it hinges on righteousness. Even though everyone is forgiven, not everyone is a new creation. At the end of all things, Jesus separates people into two groups: sheep and goats (see Matthew 25:32). Notice He separates people based on their state of being. He does not separate between dirty sheep and clean sheep. He separates between people who have the nature of sheep and those who have the nature of goats.

This additionally implies that the nature of our experience of the afterlife is a continuation of our experience in this life. Some of us have become part of the new creation; God has regenerated us, and our being belongs in the new creation. When we cross the mortal divide, we simply continue along those lines and partake in the new heaven and the new earth. Others have not become part of the new creation; their nature is part of the fallen world. Similarly, they continue to experience the old creation, as it is subjected to increasing chaos and decay for the rest of eternity. Each of us, after death, continues marching along the line of the creation to which we belong.

Question #2: Since I am already forgiven, why should I care if I sin?

Once we begin to realize we have already been forgiven, we may think it does not matter at all if we sin. If we are forgiven either way, why not, right? There is some logic in that reasoning if I am considering it from a legal point of view. But from a relational point of view, it does not make sense.

I choose not to sin because I love God and I want to follow His ways, not because I am worried about needing to obtain forgiveness afterward. In fact, if needing to obtain forgiveness afterward is what stops me from sinning, I am actually acting for myself, not for God. I am choosing not to sin because I do not want to go through the hassle of cleaning up my mess, not because my heart is drawn toward the Father and I want to live the life He wants me to live. My motivation is me, not Him.

It is our love for God and the realization that we can still hurt His heart when we sin, even if we are preemptively forgiven, that keeps us from sinning. That hurt our sin causes Him does not cause a rift in our relationship, but it does still affect Him.

This is, incidentally, why it is important to own our sin before God. We do not own it to be forgiven, because we are already forgiven. We own it in the context of our relationship. We own it because we know our sin still affects God, even if we do not need forgiveness.

Question #3: Without people needing a standard to live up to, won't they go sin-crazy?

This is a very good question—and, indeed, it is the question I mentioned at the beginning of chapter 2 that kicked off much of this journey for me. Once the Law is removed and there is no need to keep our relationship clean before God, what is to prevent us from sliding into a cesspool of debauchery?

This is why it is important that we not only be freed from the covenant of Law, but also be made righteous. If we are a new creation, our new nature—and, of course, the empowerment of the Spirit—pushes us toward good things and away from sin.

The point is that we are no longer a ticking time bomb of sin, waiting to go off. If you take a new creation and turn him or her loose to express what is in his or her heart, what will come out is not sin. This is the whole point of Paul's discussion of our now being "slaves to righteousness" in Romans 6:15–19. Our new nature prompts us to move in a holy direction, and as long as we are walking in step with the Spirit, we will be okay. As Paul says:

> But I say, walk by the Spirit, and you will not gratify the desires of the flesh.
>
> Galatians 5:16

Only if I believe I have a new nature does it seem safe to allow myself to live free from the Law. Otherwise, when I remove the constraint of having standards at which to aim, I would expect what is inside of me would be a mixed bag of good and evil.

When Jesus Comes Around

I know this chapter probably stretches your understanding—for many of us, it is a new picture of a story we thought we knew very well. What is most convincing to me about this whole picture is that it feels much more in line with the way Jesus interacted with people during His life and ministry than the picture of "repent, then be forgiven" does. How many times did Jesus require repentance before He opened the road to relationship? How many times did He hold people at arm's length until they realized the full measure of their sin? That is just not how we see Him acting.

Instead, we see Jesus acting with forgiveness almost as an assumption. Recall the story of the Prodigal Son (see Luke 15:11–32). Have you noticed the father runs to the son before the son repents to the father? Then, when the son starts to apologize, the father interrupts him and calls for a party. There is no barrier to relationship pictured here—in fact, it is just the opposite.

This is the only picture that conforms when we consider other passages, too, like when the Pharisees bring the woman caught in adultery to Jesus:

> The scribes and the Pharisees brought a woman who had been caught in adultery, and placing her in the midst they said to him, "Teacher, this woman has been caught in the act of adultery. Now in the Law, Moses commanded us to stone such women. So what do you say?"
>
> John 8:3–5

Notice the logic: This woman has sinned, and that sin needs to be dealt with. They try to pin Jesus into judgment with the Law.

But if you read the rest of the story, you will notice two things. First, Jesus does not do what the Law requires. This is incredible. As God, He did not hold the woman to the Law; rather, He freed her from its consequences. Second, He speaks to her in such a way that we know He does not even consider her need for forgiveness:

Jesus stood up and said to her, "Woman, where are they? Has no one condemned you?" She said, "No one, Lord." And Jesus said, "Neither do I condemn you; go, and from now on sin no more."

John 8:10–11

His concern is not for her forgiveness. In fact, He acts like she is already forgiven. No, His concern is for her *freedom*. He wants her to be able to live above sin.

We see Jesus acting this way over and over again in Scripture, always relating to sinners as if they are already forgiven and welcomed home. Indeed, we have a remarkable God who has already forgiven us all. This is part of the amazing news. God is not holding us away from Himself. He is welcoming us home—all of us, from the most pious to the lowliest. The Father does not see good sons and bad ones. He only sees lost sons and found sons, and His heart is that we would all come home to relationship with Him.

THINKING LIKE JESUS

- The need for forgiveness in order to restore relationship is a demand of the Law, not of God's nature. Forgiveness becomes a requirement of salvation when the Law dictates our relationship with God.
- Since Jesus is the sin sacrifice under the Law, He has granted all people forgiveness for all their sins. Every person is forgiven.
- Not everyone is saved, even though everyone is forgiven, because salvation hinges on being born again and made a new creation, not on forgiveness.

8

The Gospel
of the Kingdom

The last three chapters dug into the truth of our righteousness in Christ—a return to the original identity declared over humanity in Genesis 1:26. In this chapter, we return to the other half of the story: the restoration of the dominion of God through humanity.

As we have already seen, this is the primary message of the Gospel of the Kingdom of God, as Jesus declared and demonstrated during His ministry on earth. With the story of our righteousness fresh in hand, let's look at what the Kingdom is and how Jesus brought the return of the dominion of God through humanity.

The Essence of the Kingdom

As we turn to the subject of how Jesus introduced the Kingdom of God to us, I want to revisit a topic we discussed earlier: the nature of the word *kingdom*. Remember that when we talk about the Kingdom of God, we are not talking about the territory God rules; we are talking about the demonstration of God's rule itself. The Kingdom is not primarily a noun, meaning a place or people. It is a verb, meaning God's way of interacting with creation. It is the act of God being king.

This distinction is different from how I tend to process that term by default. When reading that Jesus spoke of the Kingdom of God being at hand, I automatically interpret it through the lens of a noun—that God is about to start His nation, the Church, on earth.

But that is not how the first-century Jews heard that phrase. They heard Jesus telling them, "God is about to prove Himself God in your life. Are you ready to experience it?"

This is why the message of the Kingdom is so often linked with signs and wonders. What does God's rule look like? It looks like the sick being healed and the demonized being set free.[1] It looks like our lives coming into the pattern God designed and that we see reflected in heaven.

Look at the language Jesus used when He sent the twelve disciples out to preach:

> "And proclaim as you go, saying, 'The kingdom of heaven is at hand.' Heal the sick, raise the dead, cleanse lepers, cast out demons. You received without paying; give without pay."
>
> Matthew 10:7–8

I used to read these verses and hear this: "Go preach the Gospel; then do these signs to prove it, so people believe you." That misses the point, though. The message and the medium are the same. The Kingdom is not present in some abstract way that is borne witness by signs and wonders. The signs and wonders *are* the Kingdom. They are God's authority in action.

Jesus was saying to go and see the Kingdom at work, then proclaim where it is acting. Go and see the Kingdom at work among the sick. Tell them the Kingdom is drawing near to them as they are healed. As you deliver the demonized, point out that the Kingdom of God is delivering them in that moment. In other words, Jesus was telling the disciples to proclaim where the Kingdom is working: "You—you're sick, but the Kingdom is drawing near to you right now in this moment. Be healed. You have been demonized, but the Kingdom is at hand, and you are being freed from demonic bondage."

It is more than the announcement of a possibility. It is the declaration of a new reality.

When it comes to the Kingdom of God, Scripture is referring to the overthrow of Satan's work and God's active intervention in the lives of the people present. Again we see it demonstrated in Matthew's gospel:

And he went throughout all Galilee, teaching in their synagogues and proclaiming the gospel of the kingdom and healing every disease and every affliction among the people.

Matthew 4:23

Jesus came not only as the redeeming Messiah, but also as the conquering King. He came bringing His Kingdom, and He introduced His Kingdom to this world. His life, death and resurrection overthrew the rule of Satan and introduced a new trajectory for history: the path of the Kingdom of God.

The Story of Jesus' Life

For a while, I wondered why the gospels spend so much time on the life of Jesus, rather than the death and resurrection of

Jesus. In terms of importance, the ratio seemed skewed. Jesus' death and resurrection are of paramount importance to us. Why, in that case, do the gospel accounts focus so much on His life and ministry?

In the gospel of Luke, 21 chapters focus on what Jesus did and taught. Only the last three chapters focus on His death and resurrection. Even John, who dedicates the most attention to the Passion, spends seventeen chapters on Jesus' life and teaching before depicting His death and resurrection in the last four.

Why this lopsided treatment? Why did the writers take so much time to share what Jesus "began to do and teach" (Acts 1:1)? These questions are merited if we do not understand that the Gospel includes the message of the Kingdom every bit as much as it does the message of our redemption.

The Gospel of the Kingdom of God holds equal weight with the message of our personal salvation. And while Jesus' death and resurrection tell the story of our righteousness, Jesus' life and ministry tell the story of how the Kingdom of God began to take hold and spread throughout all creation. The book of Acts is the story of that Kingdom work being continued in the early Church and spreading to the nations throughout the Roman Empire.

God's rule landed on planet earth in the Person of Jesus, and this is the cause into which we are all drafted. Righteousness describes who we are as we are saved; the Kingdom describes the purpose we have, now that we are saved. It is our mission statement: to extend God's rule over a creation that is out of alignment with God's original design.

What we see in the life of Jesus is what the Kingdom looks like in action. We see in Jesus that the Kingdom rules over the power of sin, as forgiveness is issued and the destructive effects of sin are overthrown as Jesus brings people to wholeness. We see the Kingdom intersects nature, as well, as water can be turned into wine or walked upon, and five loaves can be multiplied to feed a crowd. The Kingdom overcomes the power of the demonic, as countless demonized people are set free and restored to normal lives. The Kingdom overcomes the realm of sickness, as the blind see and the lame walk. The Kingdom overcomes prejudice and stigma, as we see lepers and the lame restored to functional roles in society. The Kingdom even overcomes the power of death, first as Jesus resurrects the dead and then as He enters the realm of the dead and overthrows its leader.

The life of Jesus is meant to be more for us than proof that He was God. It is a case study in the Kingdom coming, and even in how it comes. It gives us glimpses of what the task at hand looks like lived out. Now that we have been made righteous and tasked with the work of the Kingdom, what do we do? Look no further than the life of Jesus to see an example of the Kingdom lived out perfectly.

The Mission of the Church

Jesus Himself mentions the Church in only two passages. Here is the first use in all of Scripture:

> [Jesus] said to them, "But who do you say that I am?" Simon Peter replied, "You are the Christ, the Son of the living God." And Jesus answered him, "Blessed are you, Simon Bar-Jonah! For flesh and blood has not revealed this to you, but my Father who is in heaven. And I tell you, you are Peter, and on this rock I will build my *church*, and the gates of hell shall not prevail against it. I will give you the keys of the kingdom of heaven, and whatever you bind on earth shall be bound in heaven, and whatever you loose on earth shall be loosed in heaven."
>
> Matthew 16:15–19, emphasis mine

In the middle of a discussion about Jesus' identity, Simon asserts something remarkable: He believes Jesus is the Messiah. To you or me, that may seem obvious, but remember Jesus went around calling Himself the "Son of man" and *not* saying He was the Messiah. Simon believes he knows who Jesus is, and when he announces his opinion, Jesus gets excited. He is excited because He knows Simon did not think this answer up himself; rather, it came as revelation from God. The Father showed Simon Jesus' true identity. This is a signature moment, because Jesus is beginning to see that His disciples are hearing from His Father—that all the teaching and pouring into them He has done is beginning to pay off.

In response to Simon's revelation, Jesus turns around and says two things. First, He renames Simon to be called Peter. Simon sees Jesus for who He is, so Jesus does the same for him. He shows Simon he really is Peter.

More relevant for this conversation is the next portion. Jesus mentions that on the rock of the revelation of Jesus' true identity, He will build a Church, and the gates of hell will not prevail against it. His followers will be given keys to the Kingdom and will bind and loose things in relationship to earth and heaven.

Now, imagine this. The disciples have never envisioned a church. This idea has never crossed their mind. They cannot see into the 21st century and visualize people gathering in buildings and drinking coffee on Sunday mornings. All they know is that Jesus is talking about a community (the Greek word means "gathering") they have never heard of before. This gathering is a group of people that Jesus Himself is assembling, a group of people who know Jesus' true identity. The group will be so powerful that hell itself cannot stand against the onslaught the group brings. The community is granted permission to access the things of the Kingdom and to connect the will of heaven to the cry of earth, just as Jesus told His disciples to pray: His kingdom come, His will be done on earth as it is in heaven.

This is the image of the Church that Jesus gives, a group born of the revelation of Jesus, continuing to release the work of the Kingdom until hell itself caves under the power the Lord has granted them to carry.

I think Peter remembered this message and took it to heart. On the Day of Pentecost, the sermon he preaches carries a flavor reminiscent of the above passage. After connecting the events of Pentecost to a prophecy given in Joel 2, he explains it is proof Jesus was the Messiah. David prophesied of someone who would not be held down by the power of death. That person would receive the promise of the Holy Spirit and is the person David quoted in a rather confusing psalm. As Peter quotes it:

> "'The Lord said to my Lord, "Sit at my right hand, until I make your enemies your footstool."'"
>
> Acts 2:34–35

Much of Peter's sermon hangs on this passage, but it can be hard to follow. Allow me to clarify a few things. Here are Peter's words again, with my commentary in brackets:

> "'The Lord [God the Father] said to my Lord [Jesus], "Sit at my right hand [Jesus is seated at the right hand of the Father], until I make your enemies your footstool [through the Spirit being poured out on the Church]."'"

Peter is saying the Spirit is being poured out on believers because they are following Jesus. That is proof Jesus is the Messiah and that He received the promised Holy Spirit from the Father to pour out on all flesh. Now that the Spirit is being poured out on the Church, the Church is expected to continue the work of the Kingdom until every one of Jesus' enemies is brought into full submission to Him.[2]

Both in the initial description of the Church that Jesus gives in Matthew and at the conception of the Church that happened on the Day of Pentecost, the Kingdom—the mission of the Church—is brought to the forefront. The Church and the Kingdom are interlinked. There is no other mission for the Church—at least, not the Church Jesus described.

We can easily get the means and the ends confused. The Church does not exist to evangelize, to care for the poor or to study Scripture. The Kingdom can come through any of those means, but those means are not the Kingdom itself. Our assessment of effectiveness in the Church is nothing other than how much territory we have taken from the enemy.

The Commission of the Kingdom

In light of all we are talking about, the significance of the Great Commission becomes a lot clearer. Before Jesus came and brought the message and reality of the Kingdom of God, as we have already seen, the planet was under the reign of Satan. When Adam and Eve submitted their choices to Satan's input, they granted him a place of authority over them on planet earth. He snatched the keys to this planet and began to inflict his cruel will on all of creation. This is the reason Jesus referred to Satan as "the ruler of this world" (see John 12:31; 14:30; 16:11)—when Jesus was ministering on the earth, Satan's authority included the realm of the earth.

Jesus came, though, not in the line of fallen Adam but as the beginning of a new line of humanity. Paul refers to Jesus as the last Adam—a reset for humanity (see 1 Corinthians 15:45; Romans 5:12–21). Because Jesus was the only human being who did not come from the fallen line of Adam, the dominion of God that had been spoken over humanity with Adam was still applicable to Jesus. He carried the dominion of God, and, unlike Adam, He never submitted to the devil's temptations or gave that authority away. Instead, Jesus used the dominion of the Kingdom of God to challenge the rule of the devil:

> "But if it is by the Spirit of God that I cast out demons, then the kingdom of God has come upon you."
>
> Matthew 12:28

Jesus brought a challenge to the authority of the devil and defeated him at every turn. In the final attempt to end the threat Jesus presented, Satan wound up sabotaging his own kingdom and welcoming God Himself into his kingdom of death. After completing His victory over death, Jesus sent the disciples out with a new commission:

> And Jesus came and said to them, "All authority in heaven and on earth has been given to me. Go therefore and make disciples of all nations, baptizing them in the name of the Father and of the Son and of the Holy Spirit, teaching them to observe all that I have commanded you. And behold, I am with you always, to the end of the age."
>
> Matthew 28:18–20

All authority on heaven *and earth* has been given to Jesus. The authority Satan did have over the earth, Jesus now has. As a result, we are commissioned to go and reconcile every-thing—right up to the nations themselves—bringing all things into alignment with the Kingdom of God and into everything

Jesus has now made available. The Kingdom is what we are saved *to*. This is our mission on earth.

The Reality of Power

Hold on, you may be thinking. *Multiply food? Heal the sick? Cast out demons? I can't do that* . . .

When we see what the Kingdom looks like lived out, it calls us to a new level of responsibility. The target is no longer to be a "good Christian" and occasionally share our faith. Rather, each one of us is now an empowered force for God's redemption in this world. We are agents of mission, releasing God's activity on the earth through our lives.

This can be both inspiring and intimidating. What if we cannot do the things we see written in Scripture?

I see this reaction often. People believe the supernatural ministry of Jesus—healing, deliverance and so forth—is for a gifted few. You may think, *I don't have that gift. I'm not gifted to heal the sick, to prophesy or to do whatever else,* and come to the conclusion, *Others can do that. It's not for me.*

If that is what you believe, you are in good company. Jesus says the same thing about Himself! It is shared in John's gospel:

> This was why the Jews were seeking all the more to kill him, because not only was he breaking the Sabbath, but he was even calling God his own Father, making himself equal with God.
>
> So Jesus said to them, "Truly, truly, I say to you, the Son can do nothing of his own accord, but only what he sees the Father doing. For whatever the Father does, that the Son does likewise."
>
> John 5:18–19

The Jews were seeking to kill Jesus because they believed He was saying He was on par with God. But Jesus, in effect, said,

"Guys, I'm not healing the sick with My own superpowers. I don't have some amazing gift that heals the sick. This isn't Me! The miracles I work come out of cooperation with the Father. We do them together. I see what He is doing, and I join Him in His work."

For a long time, the emphasis has been on gifting. But Jesus says that anyone who believes in Him can do the same and even greater works that He did (see John 14:12). He did not say the gifted people will do the same and greater works; He said *anyone* who believes in Him will do the same and greater works. This is an invitation to all, not something reserved for a special few. This means we are all invited into the same dynamic and the same supernatural ministry He had.

Many of us draw the conclusion that we are not gifted because we have tried to do these things and it has not worked. We have prayed for the sick, and they were not healed. Or we tried to hear God for others and missed it. Thus, we draw the conclusion we are not gifted, and we shelve this kind of ministry for others. Since we have no control over our gifting, we step to the back of the line and see supernatural ministry as a calling for others.

The problem is that this response leaves what Jesus says in the dust! Surely it is not the right response. But how are we to make sense of this when it happens?

My experience is that we have understood the situation from the wrong starting point. An inability to heal the sick or prophesy does not indicate a lack of gifting. Rather, it indicates a growth curve in the area of learning to see what the Father is doing. The lack is not one of gifting but of the ability to cooperate well.

The good news is that you can learn to cooperate more effectively. If ministering in the supernatural is a gifting and we do not have that gift, we are out of luck. If, instead, it is a matter of cooperating with what God is doing, we can all learn to recognize and cooperate with God more effectively.

This is exciting news! This means the supernatural ministry of Jesus is on the table for everyone. In fact, as we learn to cooperate with the Holy Spirit, which is how the Father leads us, every gift of the Spirit is available to us—and to all believers. We just need to learn how to cooperate and do what we see the Father doing.

A few years ago, we started a class at the Vineyard Church in Urbana, Illinois, called School of Kingdom Ministry (abbreviated SoKM), in order to teach ordinary people how to minister in the power of the Holy Spirit. In that class, we teach about the Kingdom, but more than that, we break down how to see what God is doing and how to cooperate with Him—and then we practice it. Since we launched the class in 2011, it has grown and spread out to train thousands of believers across the country and around the world how to operate in supernatural ministry. We have taught teenagers and retirees how to heal the sick. Soccer moms and CEOs have learned to prophesy. People of all ages and walks of life are learning to see themselves as Jesus created them. From there, they are trained how to see what the Father is doing and to cooperate with the Spirit in the miraculous.

All around the world, I have heard this same story: "It's not for me. I don't have the gift." I cannot think of a single case where we have not been able to teach people to see what the Father is doing and to cooperate with Him in the ministry of the Spirit. Some people pick it up more quickly than others,[3] but, as Jesus said, it is on the table for all.

Listen to one person's story that shows this is true.

Jim Warner is not a pastor or a major leader in our church. He is a normal guy who works on his family's farm. Like many of us, Jim doubted it was possible for him to step into a lifestyle of miracles. He was skeptical and thought this was stuff reserved for a special, gifted few. Here is how he recounts his journey:

> About six years ago, my wife, Jo, started taking School of Kingdom Ministry. I was unable to participate with her because I worked a full-time job and helped my dad on the family farm.
>
> A few years later, the company I had worked at for 38 years downsized, and I was given a package to "retire" at the age of 57. I was happy about this because the farm was too much to handle with a full-time job, and I had seen such a change in my wife that I also wanted what she had received at School of Kingdom Ministry!
>
> That fall, I sunk my teeth into Putty's school, and my world changed. My identity changed. The way I saw God changed. As I began to explore prayer, miracles began to happen as I prayed for people.
>
> In my world before SoKM, praying for people consisted of, *Jesus, please heal X and take care of X so they can feel better*. I did this with the expectation that nothing would happen because I was unqualified. I felt powerless, even though I had witnessed healing that I thought others in our church had the gift for. I clearly did not have the "gift of healing." I would just hope someone more qualified would come along. This was from the enemy. As I began to learn my identity, my prayers began to have results!
>
> On a recent mission trip to China, my wife and I were asked to pray for people in front of the class. We were to teach them that they could pray for healing, cast out demons and prophesy. We were praying for a lady who had some demons, and she ran to the restroom. She had to throw up. We finished up with her, and she left skipping down the street! One of the pastors later informed us that he could smell the demons on her and confirmed they were gone. (Months later, I learned what demons smell like, too.) That is but one example on that trip. There were many!

I didn't realize it before, but God had been giving me information about things and people all my life. Now I began to realize that was God speaking, and I was able to cooperate with Him as He directed me.

Now that we've graduated from the class, Jo and I have continued to seek out opportunities to pray for and minister to others. We are currently participating in a prayer ministry for pastors struggling with burnout, where we regularly see restoration, physical healings and deliverances. We have also begun participating in missions and have traveled across the world to pray and minister.

I'm not a pastor, nor do I even work for the church. I still work on the farm, and in every way, I'm a normal guy. It's just that I've learned who I am in Jesus. I was a resentful skeptic. Now I truly believe Jesus is in me, and this has become my new normal.

So, if we are all able to move in the supernatural power of the Spirit, are we all supposed to do that, then? Is that the purpose of Christianity, to have everyone prophesying and casting out demons all the time? What if you feel called to something else?

The message of the Kingdom of God applies to all aspects of society. The Kingdom is bigger than healing, deliverance or prophecy. It includes financial breakthrough and social equality. It involves people growing in the wisdom of God and finding innovative solutions to the problems of society. It includes people coming into relationship with Jesus and broken families and relationships being made whole.

However, while the Kingdom is certainly broad, we also need to keep in mind that Jesus spent His time healing the sick, casting out demons and raising the dead—and He sent His disciples out to do the same. This is the starting point that leads to social and societal transformation. The first link in the chain is the miraculous, and the miraculous is meant to be woven through all facets of the Kingdom of God, redefining our world.

The Kingdom of God directs us toward many causes worth pursuing. But as we pursue the various causes of personal and social redemption and restoration, we need to remember that the method of the Kingdom is power. When Jesus rescued a bride and groom from the social embarrassment of running out of wine at their wedding, He did so with power. When Jesus fed the crowds—twice—it was with miracles, not just good organization. When He restored lepers to a functional place in society, He did this by healing them.

Jesus modeled a power-infused ministry in every realm of society. This "method of the Kingdom" is important to keep in mind as we pursue whatever cause to which we feel specifically called. As Paul says:

> For the kingdom of God does not consist in talk but in power.
>
> 1 Corinthians 4:20

If you feel called to heal the sick and cast out demons, that is great! Pursue that with the power of God. If you feel called to combat the evils of prejudice, that is fantastic. Do so with the means of the Kingdom; may God prophetically guide you in how to go about it, and may His power manifest so you can tear down strongholds in people. If you feel called to the realm of business, that is wonderful! I pray God speaks to your innovations and strategies, that your business would be a light in the darkness and that God would supernaturally generate wealth through you for Kingdom purposes.

Of course, in whatever sphere we operate, may we all be equipped to pray for those around us who have needs and to offer the Lord's healing touch and prophetic insight.

This is the call we all share: that we would be an active part of God's Kingdom working redemptively on this planet. Jesus has purchased a new heaven and a new earth, and now He looks to you and me, the Church, to partner with the Holy Spirit to bring every enemy of His to bow as a footstool under His rule.

THINKING LIKE JESUS

- Jesus' life demonstrates the message of the Kingdom of God: that God is redemptively working on the earth through believers.
- The mission of the Kingdom of God is the true purpose of the Church. The Holy Spirit has been poured out on believers so we can continue the Kingdom work Jesus started.
- The supernatural ministry of Jesus is available in all realms of society and is something in which we can all learn to operate, as we learn to do what we see the Father doing.

9

Christ in Us

Saint Patrick was a man of incredible faith and one whom God used powerfully to reach the Irish people. While today the holiday that bears his name is mostly associated with a day of drunkenness, there is good reason for this saint to be remembered more than fifteen hundred years after his death.

Born in Britain sometime between AD 385–387, Patrick was raised in a Christian family. As a teenager, he was captured by Irish pirates and forced to work as a slave and sheepherder for a high priest of Druidism, the predominant form of paganism the Irish practiced at that time.

Patrick leaned into God during his six years of enslavement, practicing nearly constant prayer. He was eventually able to escape the slavery and, after an adventurous journey, was reunited with his family.

He pursued religious education and one day had a dream where a man named Victorious came and handed him a letter titled "The Voice of the Irish." As Patrick read the letter in the dream, he was forced to stop reading because he was so moved by the voice of the Irish that asked him to return and evangelize them. This became his goal, and eventually the pope sent him to spread the Good News in Ireland.

Patrick lived the rest of his life in Ireland and was powerfully used by God to reach the Irish people. In fact, the reason he is celebrated with a holiday is that he almost single-handedly introduced the Christian faith to the Irish people. He brought multitudes to faith and walked in great power. Some of the accounts of the signs and wonders worked in his ministry are pretty awe-inspiring. Here is just one example:

> For the blind and the lame, the deaf and the dumb, the palsied, the lunatic, the leprous, the epileptic, all who labored under any disease, did he in the Name of the Holy Trinity restore unto the power of their limbs and unto entire health; and in these good deeds was he daily practiced. Thirty and three dead men, some of whom had been many years buried, did this great reviver raise from the dead, as above we have more fully recorded.[1]

My favorite part is the almost nonchalant mention of his resurrecting people who had been dead for many years!

How did Patrick learn to walk in such power? Clearly, he was a man of deep prayer, which I suspect was part of it. There is a famous prayer he wrote, called "Saint Patrick's Breastplate," that he would pray for protection and empowerment against the pagan powers and magicians with whom he constantly interacted. The prayer includes a meditation on Christ's presence in his life:

> Christ with me, Christ before me, Christ behind me,
> Christ in me, Christ beneath me, Christ above me,
> Christ on my right, Christ on my left,
> Christ when I lie down, Christ when I sit down,
> Christ in the heart of every man who thinks of me,

Christ in the mouth of every man who speaks of me,
Christ in the eye that sees me,
Christ in the ear that hears me.[2]

Saint Patrick was connected to the reality that Christ lived within him and that Jesus was walking every day alongside him. This was not a quaint idea to Patrick; it was a reality to which he was connected, one he experienced and that framed the way he lived his life.

Too often, we have no connection to this powerful truth. It is abstract and distant from our experience, and we cannot picture it having any relevance to our everyday lives. This is a great shame, because the reality that Christ lives within us is not meant to be a comforting theology, but an invitation to live on a new level.

Christ Lives Your Life

The apostle Paul was in touch with this same reality of Christ living within him. In fact, he described it as a cornerstone of the Gospel:

I have been crucified with Christ. It is no longer I who live, but Christ who lives in me. And the life I now live in the flesh I live by faith in the Son of God, who loved me and gave himself for me.

Galatians 2:20

In addition to seeing himself as dead to sin and living every moment in faith, Paul knew he no longer was the one living his life. Instead, Christ was living through him. In both letters to the Corinthians, Paul wrote that he expected them to be in touch with this reality, too, and to live from this same starting point:

For when one says, "I follow Paul," and another, "I follow Apollos," are you not being merely human?

1 Corinthians 3:4

Or do you not realize this about yourselves, that Jesus Christ is in you?

2 Corinthians 13:5

Paul expected the Corinthians to realize they were not "merely human." In fact, Jesus lived within them and wanted them to act accordingly. This truth was to be the starting point for all their actions and how they lived their lives.

We can live from that same starting point—and if we do, it changes everything. Think about it. If God is living in you, what else matters? Does anything hold a candle to the reality of God Himself living in and through you? Of course not!

So, why does that not feel more real to us?

There are at least two reasons. The first is because we are not clear on the righteousness that has been given to us. The second is because we have not spent much time thinking about or exploring this idea.

The reality of our righteousness—the fact that we are fully dead to sin and that God has regenerated our humanity to match the original template intended for us of the image and likeness of God—is foundational if we want to come in contact with the reality of Jesus dwelling within us. But we cannot access this reality if our perception of our righteousness stands on shaky ground. If we see ourselves as a "house divided," with a nature that wars against itself, then we will relegate the reality of Christ dwelling within us to an abstract concept. We will know God is holy and pure but believe ourselves incongruent with that standard, and how can we expect to experience a reality that does not make sense to us? We pile it up with a number of other theological truths that are mysterious to us. We tell ourselves God sees Himself living in us, but we do not have any expectation to find Him there ourselves.

If, however, we recognize that God has cleansed us and made us brand new, holy and pure, then we can begin to see ourselves as fit vessels for Him to dwell inside. The work of Christ that has dealt with our sinful nature has made us into the kind of temple the Lord finds appealing. Jesus really did cleanse the temple of all its corruption—a symbol of our being cleansed—and God's Spirit dwells within us now. We know this is not a metaphor but a reality. He has made His home in us!

Christ Unites Humanity and Divinity

What does it mean for God to live in us, then? It means you are not the only one inside of you.

What a very strange thought.

But in fact, if you are to take Galatians 2:20 as it reads, then you must come to believe there is more of God in you than there is *you* in you! Paul says:

> I have been crucified with Christ. *It is no longer I who live, but Christ who lives in me.* And the life I now live in the flesh I live by faith in the Son of God, who loved me and gave himself for me.
>
> Galatians 2:20, emphasis mine

Think about that. There is more God in you right now than you in you.

But what does it mean to live with two beings inside of you? How do you make contact with that reality?

One of the first things this does is redefine what it means to be human. Many of us carry an assumption that our humanity is opposed to God's divinity—that humanity and divinity are like oil and water; they do not mix. Our goal, when we believe this way, is that of submitting our humanity to God's divinity. We pray things like, *Less of me and more of You, Lord*.

But this kind of thinking, which pits our humanity against God's deity, is unhelpful and a roadblock that needs to be overcome. Our humanity is not opposed to God's divinity; remember, we were made in His image and likeness. Rather, our humanity is a *vehicle of expression* of God's divinity. It is not something God tries to work around. It is something He wants to work through.

In Jesus, everything that God is was put into a human body. Everything! No part of God was left out, and no part of God was constrained when Jesus became human. Paul says, "For in him [Jesus] the whole fullness of deity dwells bodily" (Colossians 2:9).

Think about that. God does not fit in the room you may be sitting in right now. God does not fit in your city or on this planet. God does not fit in the entire universe. And yet He fits inside a human—every part of Him, every last bit, the whole fullness of Him does.

To further clarify, let's consider a contrasting example. Pardon the oddness of this example, but it was the closest illustration I could think of. Suppose you had a dog you were really attached to. This dog was such a good friend that you wanted to experience relationship with that dog even more. Suppose, as well, that science had made it possible to transplant you from your human body into a dog's body.

If you chose to do that, elements of yourself would need to be left behind. A dog cannot carry your capacity for rational thought. A dog cannot hope or dream the way you do. A dog does not have the creative capacities you have or the ability to steward resources like you can. You would have to leave behind major elements of who you are in order to become a dog.

Yet when God became a human being, He did not leave *anything* behind. Nothing at all. No part of Him was sacrificed or dropped when Jesus became God incarnate.

Most of us think of God as a level profoundly above us. We are the dog to His human. And yet Scripture points to the opposite. This is what it means when Scripture teaches we not only carry His image but are *like God* (see Genesis 1:26). Our humanity has been created to fit God. We are made in the same "shape" He is.

Strong's concordance defines the word *likeness* in Genesis 1:26 as "resemblance; concretely, model, shape."[3] We were made with God's model, God's shape. It is like we are a glove His divinity fills. We are specially designed for His hand. We have all the fingers in all the right places, and His divinity is made to fill and animate our humanity, with no facet left out.

Many of us are not at peace with facets of ourselves. We think our emotions hold us back. We do not see ourselves as relational enough, or we see ourselves as too relational. We do not love the shape our body takes.

The important thing to realize is that each and every aspect of who we are exists as something God has, too. The reason you have emotions is that God has emotions. You have relationships because God does. You have a physical frame because that reveals something of God. You have finances, rational thought, hopes and dreams, a will, a spirit and everything else because God does. Each and every one of the slices of your life exists because each and every one is a "finger" on God's hand, so to speak.

Our journey is one of discovering the God who lives in us through the mold of our humanity. It is our humanity that God fills and uses to reveal His image.

This is how we make peace with ourselves. It is a part of the journey of coming to know God. You have emotions because God does, but what would it be like for God to feel His emotions through you? What would it be like for God to live out relationship through you? For God to think His thoughts within you? For you to experience God within your physical frame?

I love to be in nature. It is refreshing and rejuvenating to my soul, and I carve out time to walk in the beauty of God's creation as often as I am able. Since I live in central Illinois, which is devoid of mountains and beaches, I often immerse myself in the woods. There is a forest preserve about fifteen minutes from my house, and I often stop there on my way home from work and spend time walking about or reflecting on what may be coming up next.

One day, as I was walking there, I was struck by how good it is for me to spend time in the woods. I remember asking the Lord, *Why is it that I like walking in the woods so much?*

Ever have one of those times when God answers back with actual words? That does not happen to me every day, but sometimes it does. This was one of those times. I felt the Lord reply, *What makes you think you're the one enjoying them here? I'm the One who made them.*

Mind. Blown.

Here I was, thinking the woods were rejuvenating to *me*, and the Lord revealed He was looking through my eyes and enjoying—through me—the creation He called good. I just got to enjoy the by-product of being a part of that process.

Ever since that day, I have felt God so much more involved in my life than I previously realized. He is in me, living through me every day.

He intends to live through you in the same way.

Have you ever noticed that hearing God often feels fuzzy and subjective—that as we learn to recognize His voice, it becomes difficult to distinguish whether a thought is from Him or from us? The line gets fuzzy because we are more intertwined with the Lord than we think. Paul says:

> But he who is joined to the Lord becomes one spirit with him.
>
> 1 Corinthians 6:17

We can struggle to differentiate between our thoughts and God's because we experience God's thoughts in our mind.[4] God does not navigate around our humanity to interact with us. He uses it. Our humanity is a perfectly designed vehicle for that purpose.

This means the whole of our life can be a path to discover God and a map to reveal Him. We can expect to discover the Lord in every facet of ourselves. The relevant question is this: Are you looking for Him there?

Rather than being at odds with your hopes and dreams, what if you accepted that having hopes and dreams is a part of being human and began to ask the Lord to reveal what He is hoping and dreaming in you? What if your hopes and dreams have as much to do with His heart as they do yours? What if they have *more* to do with His heart? If we come to peace with ourselves, we can begin to see God using our humanity to draw us closer into relationship with Him.

The journey is not just one of relationship, though. It is also one of stewardship. Once we begin to connect with the Lord's hopes and dreams in us, that portion of our humanity has an opportunity to enflesh God. Our life becomes a living picture of what God is like.

This is true for every element of our humanity. We live not only our relationships, but God's through us. We think not only our thoughts, but God's, as well. We steward not only our resources, but also God's. Our life—the whole of it—becomes a living picture of who God is.

In some sense, you could say that while Jesus was fully *the* incarnation, God has also granted us to become *an* incarnation. God has taken up residence within us. As we live yielded to Him, in connection with Him through trust, or faith, God lives His life through us. (This is the second portion of Galatians 2:20 in action—when we live by faith, it is not our life we live, but Christ's.)

Here is the completion of our original design: to bear God's image and likeness to the rest of creation. We are a living, breathing, flesh-and-blood picture of what God is like. We reveal His nature through the life we live in this world.

We Experience God's Attributes

This means God's attributes, who God is, should not just be a set of ideas we learn. Rather, they are an invitation for an experience we are meant to step into. This is what Peter meant in a passage that sounds so extreme, it is hard to know what to make of it:

> His divine power has granted to us all things that pertain to life and godliness, through the knowledge of him who called us to his own glory and excellence, by which he has granted to us his precious and very great promises, so that through them you may become partakers of the divine nature, having escaped from the corruption that is in the world because of sinful desire.
>
> 2 Peter 1:3–4

Peter says everything we need has been granted to us through a growing relationship with God. As the relationship grows, we partake of God's nature. We do not *become* God, but we get to experience what being God is like. We live our lives as if we have not only our nature, but His, as well.

A study of the attributes of God can take place in an abstract, logical kind of way: God is portrayed as omnipotent (all-powerful), omnipresent (present in all places) and so forth. Theologians enumerate His attributes as a description of His nature.

While I do believe there is value in this kind of study, I think it largely misses the point. God reveals Himself and relates to us *relationally*. His Son came as a person, someone we could relate to, not as an abstract idea. This means the attributes of God are not meant to exist within the structure of logic. They are meant to be something we experience through our relationship with Him.

Believe it or not, we can come to participate in the omnipotence of God:

> And Jesus said to him, "'If you can'! All things are possible for one who believes."
>
> Mark 9:23

And Paul seemed connected to some form of God's omnipresence in this statement:

> When you are assembled in the name of the Lord Jesus and my spirit is present, with the power of our Lord Jesus, you are to deliver this man to Satan for the destruction of the flesh, so that his spirit may be saved in the day of the Lord.
>
> 1 Corinthians 5:4–5

Honestly, I am not sure what to make of what Paul is saying here, other than to say he believed some part of himself could be present with the Corinthians, even if he was not with them physically.

The point is this: God invites us to participate in Himself to such an extent that we experience life like we are Him. This is what it means to be a "son of God." Remember, to the Jew, calling yourself a son of God made a statement not just about your relationship to God, but also your likeness to God in nature:

> This was why the Jews were seeking all the more to kill him [Jesus], because not only was he breaking the Sabbath, but he was even calling God his own Father, *making himself equal with God.*
>
> John 5:18, emphasis mine

This may stretch you as you read this. I understand. It stretches me. This is something I struggle to believe. If the Bible did not say it, I would throw it out. But it does say it! Again, we must learn to align our lives with what Scripture says, even if it does not (yet) match our experience, because it is God's truth, not our own.

The early Church was much more in touch with this concept. Many of the early Church fathers wrote about it, and in a more extreme way than I am suggesting here. For instance:

Irenaeus (130–202): God became what we are in order to make us what He is Himself.

Clement of Alexandria (150–215): He who obeys the Lord and follows the prophecy given through Him becomes a god while still moving about in the flesh.

Athanasius (296–373): The Word was made flesh in order that we might be made gods. Just as the Lord became a man, so also we are deified through His flesh and inherit everlasting life.

Augustine (354–430): To make human beings gods, He who was God was made man.

I will be honest with you. I am uncomfortable with some of the things these men said. I can push myself to accept that we get to partake in God's nature—but saying we become gods feels like taking it too far to me![5]

Honestly, though, Jesus said almost this exact thing, quoting Psalm 82, when the Jews objected to His claiming likeness with God by calling Himself God's Son:

> The Jews answered him, "It is not for a good work that we are going to stone you but for blasphemy, because you, being a man, make yourself God." Jesus answered them, "Is it not written in your Law, 'I said, you are gods'? If he called them gods to whom the word of God came—and Scripture cannot be broken—do you say of him whom the Father consecrated and sent into the world, 'You are blaspheming,' because I said, 'I am the Son of God'?"
>
> John 10:33–36

Jesus says those who received the Word of God are gods. Not even *sons* of God, but gods themselves. I have a difficult time with this, but apparently the line between God and ourselves blurs a lot more than any of us realize.

Jesus, as the incarnation, is a picture of what we are becoming. In Him, humanity and divinity permanently united, never to be separated again. As we become one spirit with Him, the same begins to happen in us. God's divinity begins to unite with our humanity, and we take on the same quality of enfleshing who God is.

In this sense, we are fit to be the Bride of Christ. We take on the same nature and character as Jesus did. Jesus will not be unequally yoked. His bride will take on the same quality He did: God enfleshed in humanity, the visible image of the invisible God.

I remember a time this became real to me. I was roughhousing with my oldest daughter one day on our bed because she loves to wrestle and play.

At one point, I pushed off the bed with my arms to stand up. As I did, I felt two of the vertebrae in my lower back pull apart and then come back together in about a second. It was an odd sensation, and I knew something bad was underway.

As soon as the vertebrae came back together, my lower back locked up with severe tension and pain. As my mind listed off the various injuries I could have experienced, maybe a slipped disk or a pinched nerve—*Oh no, will I need surgery?*—I hobbled to the living room, unable to bend my back.

I told my wife what happened and asked if she would get a heating pad so I could try to relax the muscles in my back. She went to the other room to get it, and I tried to sit down on the couch. To sit down, I sort of dropped onto the sofa. I could not control myself well enough to let myself down easily.

When I began to lean back, I had an epiphany. *Hold on,* I thought. *Jesus lives in me.* It was not a thought I was trying to summon, but rather a simple realization, like, *Oh yeah. He's in there.*

It was the only thought in my mind for that moment. It was the most real thing—the only real thing—for that sliver of time.

By the time my seat hit the sofa, at least 90 percent of the pain in my back was gone. I had mobility. Other than some muscle tightness, my back felt strong and stable.

I was stunned at what had just happened. In a second of being connected to God's presence inside me in a real way, my back had been repaired. I sat with the heating pad for a while to loosen up the tight muscles but had no further pain or problems.

Now, do not make the mistake of thinking this is my everyday experience. It is not. But I am committed to keep growing in touch with the way God wants to fill my humanity with His divinity.

God lives in His people. This is a powerful reality when we begin to get in touch with it.

THINKING LIKE JESUS

- God wants to incarnate and indwell our humanity. Every part of our humanity is designed to be a vessel God can take and fill and express Himself through.
- This is an invitation to relationally experience God living through us. When God lives through our humanity, we experience Him in profound and dynamic ways.

10

Living from the Inside Out

One of my favorite movies released in the last few years is Disney-Pixar's *Inside Out*. The movie is set in the head of an eleven-year-old girl named Riley and is an exploration of how our inner life determines the way we interact with the world around us. Riley's emotions—Joy, Anger, Fear, Disgust and Sadness—are delightfully personified. I have yet to get through the climactic scene toward the end without crying.

What I love about the movie is how true it rings to our experience. Like Riley, we all live on the interface between two worlds: the world around us and the world within us. At first glance, we might think the world around us is vast and extensive and that the world of our thoughts, emotions and hopes is less pervasive. I do not believe that is the case. I find our inner world to be as dynamic and complex as the one in which we eat, drink and breathe.

Furthermore, when we give our lives to Jesus and He births us anew, our inner world becomes the starting point for the Kingdom's work in our lives. Jesus removes our heart of stone and gives us a heart of flesh. He puts His Spirit within us. God works first to remodel our inner world and then to shape the world around us. The Kingdom comes through the remodeling of our inner lives:

> For the kingdom of God is not a matter of eating and drinking but of righteousness and peace and joy in the Holy Spirit.
>
> Romans 14:17

This idea connects to an important question we have not yet considered: How does the Kingdom come through us? Thus far, we have looked at how we are saved (chapter 5) and what it means to grow (chapter 6), and we have discussed the results of being saved in the world around us (chapters 8 and 9). But how are those results energized? What causes us to be able to release the Kingdom of God in this world? What empowers us to live in such a way that God enfleshes Himself in our humanity?

We are energized by a biblical idea that confuses many of us: faith.

Living by Faith

The term *faith* is used many different ways in the Christian life. We use it to refer to the tenets of what we believe, meaning "the Christian faith." We say the salvation process is something that occurs only by faith. When people rely on God's promises in trying situations, we say they are standing in faith. Faith is often also connected to the idea of righteousness. "Righteousness by faith" is often contrasted with "righteousness by works," and rightfully so. This panoply of uses often blurs what the term means.

Paul clarifies the role of faith in the life of a believer in an interesting, albeit tough to untangle, verse in Romans 1:

For I am not ashamed of the gospel, for it is the power of God
for salvation to everyone who believes, to the Jew first and also
to the Greek. For in it the righteousness of God is revealed from
faith for faith, as it is written, "The righteous shall live by faith."

Romans 1:16–17

Wow! That second part of the passage, about how the righteousness of God is revealed "from faith for faith," is kind of
a mouthful. No wonder we tend to depend on the first part
of the passage. What does "from faith for faith" even mean?

It provides us with an important application of the word
faith. Let's break it down (with my comments, once again,
offered in brackets):

For in it [the Gospel] the righteousness of God is revealed [God
has made His righteousness available to us through the Gospel]
from faith [righteousness flows to us from faith and is available to
us as we turn to God in faith; we are made new by faith in Him,
not by our performance] for faith [but righteousness also leads
us to faith; as new creations, faith rises in our hearts; faith leads
us to righteousness, and righteousness leads us to more faith].

Many of us have not thought much about this portion of
the passage—how it is saying righteousness not only comes to
us *by* faith but also brings us *to* faith. I think of it like rungs
of a ladder: Faith reveals to us righteousness, which grows our
faith, which reveals to us even more of our righteousness, which
grows our faith even more. This cycle is meant to carry us on
an upward trajectory in the things of God.

In other words, faith is not something we have only at our
salvation event. It also becomes a lifestyle for us. It becomes
how we live all the time. This is why Paul closed the passage by
saying, "The righteous shall live by faith." He does not say the

righteous *will be alive* by faith, which would refer to salvation, but the righteous *shall live by* faith. Every day is meant to be another day of faith for the righteous.

So, faith is the natural heart posture of a new creation. I find this fascinating, because we often work hard to avoid being in places that require faith! We work and plan and strategize and do everything we can to keep from coming to the end of ourselves. Many of us turn to God only as a last resort. He is our "Hail Mary" option, someone we seek out only in the most dire of circumstances, when there are no other options before us.

This means we have a long way to go to renew our minds. Dependence on God—faith—is meant to be normal for us now. Only our lack of belief in God's goodness and our lack of trust in His faithfulness keep us dependent on ourselves.

Living with Confidence

If faith is meant to be a lifestyle for us, then we need to know when we are in faith or not in faith. We need to know when we are living it and when we are not.

Unfortunately, we often think of faith as something akin to confidence. Have you ever seen someone living from a place of faith? They seem so bold, so confident. They are sure of what is going to happen. But you know what? That surety is the *product* of faith, not the essence of it. We go wrong when we think their confidence is their faith.

This is an important distinction because seeing other people's confidence and calling it faith may cause us to try to summon confidence for ourselves. We may try to create boldness and assurance for ourselves. We might seek to replicate the inner position we see in their outer person—but it does not work. We cannot create our own faith. And the confidence that comes from having faith is not the same road that leads us to gaining faith.

Fortunately, Scripture defines *faith* for us. Of the few biblical terms explicitly defined in Scripture, *faith* is one of them:

> Now faith is the assurance of things hoped for, the conviction of things not seen.
>
> Hebrews 11:1

Notice there are two parts of faith listed here: the effect of faith and the essence of faith. The "assurance of things hoped for" is the effect, meaning the result. The result of faith is confidence. It is where faith leads us.

The other part—the essence of faith—is captured in the second portion of the verse: "the conviction of things not seen." This part is not about confidence. It is about perception. We experience conviction when our heart sees, or perceives, something. This is like what happens when we experience the conviction of sin; when the reality of sin settles in our heart, we see it in a way we never have before.

Faith takes that same seeing of the heart and directs it at the unseen realm. In other words, faith happens when the reality of our heart is in touch with the Spirit realm. It happens when the unseen realm becomes more real to us than the visible realm. When we perceive that reality and that reality becomes our truth, we are in faith.

The rest of Hebrews 11 draws this point out. Let me draw your attention to a few of the highlights:

> By faith we understand that the universe was created by the word of God, so that *what is seen was not made out of things that are visible.*
>
> verse 3, emphasis mine

By faith Noah, being warned by God *concerning events as yet unseen*, in reverent fear constructed an ark for the saving of his household.

verse 7, emphasis mine

These all died in faith, not having received the things promised, *but having seen them and greeted them from afar*, and having acknowledged that they were strangers and exiles on the earth.

verse 13, emphasis mine

By faith he [Moses] left Egypt, not being afraid of the anger of the king, *for he endured as seeing him who is invisible.*

verse 27, emphasis mine

The great deeds of faith started with a heart perception. That heart perception created an assurance of the things hoped for. The assurance is a product of the unseen reality we perceive when we are in faith—an assurance that comes from knowing our Kingdom is unshakable.

If someone is in a place of faith, they may look bold from the outside, but they do not usually feel as if they are acting boldly. Their boldness is a natural by-product of their faith. Their confidence is innate, given their starting point: the conviction of things not seen.

Living in Truth

What does this look like lived out? All this theology is well and good, but how does it change our life?

As believers, we are meant to live in a reality where the unseen realm and the truths of the Spirit are at the forefront of our heart all the time. They are the truths we connect to, the reality we walk in step with. This has profound implications for our experience of life because it changes the way life flows to us.

Our inner world is designed to be plugged in to something. You can shape it and take control of it to some extent, but you were designed to be in relationship with God. There is a part of you that is made to be in relational connection and to take cues of truth from something outside yourself.

Every one of us needs an identity. We need a way to think of ourselves and to understand the value we have and where it comes from. We are meant to be plugged in to something—to draw life, security, value and significance from something.

God designed it so the majority of these deep needs get met through our parents when we are young. We are supposed to feel safe because of their care. As we age, we develop a sense of self that is independent from our family of origin, but we are still meant to get these needs met through connection with something.

As we grow up, we learn the pattern of this world. The words of others become a form of truth to us. When others critique us, we are unable to dismiss it and shrug it off. When we get cut off in traffic, we lose our cool for an hour. When a friend suggests a restaurant, we try it.

We operate in these ways because, before we come to faith in Christ, it is the only option available to us. We are plugged in to the world around us. We cannot help but look to the world to give us something. Our sense of worth is connected to the messages others send us, and we take those messages as truth.

The problem with this is that it chains our inner experience to the world. If things line up well, we have a good day. When things head a different direction, we get taken out. We spend a lot of our time and energy arranging the environment around us to control the environment within us. Our prayers focus on asking God to change things so we can be okay.

Faith begins to lift us above that level of existence. As we connect with the realities of the Spirit in meaningful ways, we are freed from the need to be plugged in to this world. Our worth and our value derive from Jesus, not the opinions of others. Our cues no longer come from the situations around us, but from the Spirit within us.

Ultimately, we are meant to be connected to and in relationship with Jesus. Jesus provides us with the sense of significance, security, value and life we seek, and He invites us into that life when we come to Him.

The extent to which we do not get those needs met in Jesus is the extent to which we will try to find other ways to meet them. Maybe it is a sense of self-worth that comes through a career or a sense of value or protection that comes from a relationship. Maybe we try to draw a sense of viability from a social life, a hobby or a destructive habit, like pornography or gambling.

The truth is, any area of life where our needs get met outside of Jesus is an idol to us. But when we try to meet those needs through idols, our life does not work very well. This is because idols are unable to meet our needs in a sustainable way. The sense of significance we gain from our career will only satisfy us temporarily; soon we will need to conquer another hill or meet another goal to feel significant again. A destructive habit or a relationship can only remind us of our value or grant us a sense of vitality for a period of time; soon we become empty and need another dose.

But beyond the temporary high these idols offer us, we have a second problem. When those idols are threatened, we panic. We need those idols to be okay because our significance and value are tied to them. If our career gets threatened, we are not just faced with losing a career; we are also faced with losing our sense of significance or value. It presents us with an identity crisis.

For instance, have you ever lost your cool when someone cut you off in traffic? A person who interrupts our commute can ruin our whole morning. How can someone we do not even know, and who likely did not do it on purpose, hold such power over us? Those knee-jerk reactions are, again, the result of our needs being threatened.

We lose our cool when we are cut off in traffic when we are not established in our value. When someone cuts us off, they send us the message, "I matter more than you." If we get our value from the opinions or thoughts of others, our value just went out the window when they moved into our lane. It is not about being a few seconds late to where we are going. It is about being reduced to worthlessness. When our value is taken from us, we react in anger and point the finger at the other person, but the problem is in us. We are the ones not established in the truth or deriving our value from Jesus.

What happens when someone in tune with the identity Jesus grants us gets cut off? Before anything happens, they are operating from a different mindset. The Holy Spirit has renewed their mind. Their value is not up for grabs. They think God's thoughts and opinions about themselves. Their inner reality says, *God, I'm excited You think I'm worth relating to. I'm glad You're my Dad and think I'm significant. It's great to know I'm special to You.*

When a person rooted in this truth gets cut off, their response is different because they do not feel or think anything has been taken from them. The message "I matter more than you" is received differently because they do not need to hear the message "You matter" from anyone else. Their feathers do not get ruffled. If anything, their response is one of compassion: *God, I ask You to bless that person. They don't see me as I really am—they don't see the value I have before You. They probably need to show themselves they're better than others to be okay. God, bring them into Your truth. Show them they have value before You and that they don't need to take it from others to gain it for themselves.*

This is the power of understanding we have been made new. Because God no longer believes we are broken, we can be open to Him and get our emotional needs met through Him.

As we have already explored in depth, many of us see ourselves as forgiven but still losers. We think God does not like us because He should not like us. We see ourselves as stacked full of sin, which we know is the antithesis of God's nature. How could we expect to experience a close relationship with God when we believe some part of our being is wired to oppose God at the core?

As a result, we see ourselves through a negative lens. We believe we are messed up and broken. We are not what we wish we could be. This negative self-image only magnifies the need to draw significance and life from something or someone else, often with disastrous results. It is a sad irony, but generally the more sinful we see ourselves, the more idols we worship to fill the hole in our self-image.

It took a long time for me to open up to seeing myself in a new way. It took a long time for me to believe I was no longer a sinner, but a righteous new creation who has value because God gave it to me. It was a scary journey for me, but never has a journey in faith been more significant or freeing.

I admonish you to leave behind the picture of yourself as a loser, a failure and a sinner. You are not any of those things anymore—and not because of yourself, but because of Jesus. Depend on Him for your very identity. This is the starting point of living in faith.

Living in a New Reality

This is the kind of thinking Paul outlines in Romans 8:31–39, when he says:

What then shall we say to these things? If God is for us, who can be against us? He who did not spare his own Son but gave him up for us all, how will he not also with him graciously give us all things? Who shall bring any charge against God's elect? It is God who justifies. Who is to condemn? Christ Jesus is the one who died—more than that, who was raised—who is at the right hand of God, who indeed is interceding for us. Who shall separate us from the love of Christ? Shall tribulation, or distress, or persecution, or famine, or nakedness, or danger, or sword? As it is written,

> "For your sake we are being killed all the day long;
> we are regarded as sheep to be slaughtered."

No, in all these things we are more than conquerors through him who loved us. For I am sure that neither death nor life, nor angels nor rulers, nor things present nor things to come, nor powers, nor height nor depth, nor anything else in all creation, will be able to separate us from the love of God in Christ Jesus our Lord.

These are not platitudes meant for our fridge or computer wallpaper that simply make us feel better. They are an invitation into a new way of thinking that is rooted in the things of the Spirit.

Paul is arguing that the Gospel adds up to a new reality. When he says God is for us, he is saying our focus is meant to be on that. If someone takes a position against us, that does not change that God is for us. It only positions the other person against God.

What about lack? What about those times when it seems we do not have enough of the time, resources or energy we need? Not a problem. Paul says God graciously gives us all things, and God's gifts to us are unceasing. In the spiritual realm, God not only gave us the greatest gift, but He continues to give to us everything we need. If we are living connected to that truth, lack can never threaten us.

What if we are accused of wrongdoing? Paul says it is God who justifies us. We should tell those people, "Go for it. You are only going to run into my heavenly defense attorney. I will let you and God sort that one out. He says my sin is separated as far as the east is from the west."

Is someone interested in finding fault with us? Paul says no one can condemn us—and, furthermore, that Jesus intercedes for us. Tell that person, "Take it up with Jesus. I died and resurrected with Him. He has made me spotless and brand new. In fact, He is praying for me at this very moment. If you are committed to undoing the work Jesus has done in me, I will let you and God sort that out. I'm going to keep my focus on who Jesus has made me to be. If you're interested in encouraging that journey, I am all ears. If you want to tear me down, take it up with Him."

Last of all, what has the capacity to divide us from the reality of the love of Christ that shapes our inner experience? Do any of the things Paul listed toward the end of this passage—which, in fact, Paul faced regularly—force us out of that reality? No. In any of our external challenges, we are more than conquerors. A conqueror is someone who battles and wins, but someone who is *more* than a conqueror does not even have to fight. That is the reality we are invited to live in. We do not have to fight against the battles on the outside of us because we live on a plane of reality far above them.

Does this mean we will never have problems? Of course not. That is not what Paul is saying. He is saying the problems we face will not shake or rattle us. We will still have things to figure out and situations we would rather not face, but those things no longer have the capacity to control our inner world. They do not shape our experience of life. Our inner world is now shaped by one thing, and one thing only:

For I am sure that neither death nor life, nor angels nor rulers, nor things present nor things to come, nor powers, nor height nor depth, nor anything else in all creation, will be able to separate us from the love of God in Christ Jesus our Lord.

Romans 8:38–39

The love of God, as revealed in Jesus, is the most powerful reality for us. Nothing else can cut us off from that. We may let ourselves get distracted, and we may be on a learning curve of how to stay connected to God's love in our present situations, but nothing must force us out of that reality.

Whatever situation you face right now, God's love for you is a more powerful reality, and it is one into which the Spirit wants to guide you. You can live in joy and peace in the midst of your challenges. You can sleep through the storm like Jesus did. The Lord can prepare for you a table in the presence of your enemies. It is possible to live this way.

Living into Holiness

The theme of suffering in the life of a believer is a common thread in the New Testament. With the backdrop of the line of thinking we have developed here, we can begin to see why.

Let me start by saying I do not believe there is inherent value in suffering. God is not causing us to suffer to toughen us up. The issue at hand is not even our character, although our character can grow through suffering. No, suffering is an opportunity to practice living from the inside out.

You might say suffering is like strength training for living from your inner reality. When a weight lifter wants to bulk up muscles, he or she will lift maximum weight with a small number of repetitions. This tears down the muscles so the body can rebuild them stronger and bigger than before.

In the same way, suffering is a maximum-resistance situation for our inner world. It trains us to draw from the world within instead of taking cues from the world outside. As such, when suffering is a part of our lives, God desires to use that suffering to strengthen our ability to stay rooted in our connection to His reality.

Few subjects cast a shadow on the character of our Father more than the suffering and the discipline of the Lord do. Let me hasten to add the following disclaimer: I do not believe God sends suffering into our lives. He does not need to. Plenty of suffering happens without Him sending it to us. I do not believe He aims pain at His children. It is not within His heart to do that.

When suffering enters our lives, it is an indicator of one of two things. First, it can be caused by agents other than God. Sickness and poverty are tools of the enemy, and, as we have already seen, the enemy has free will, just like we do. Additionally, we make choices that inflict suffering upon each other.

Second, we can suffer because of a lack of faith. Unbelief is uncomfortable. God has promised to provide for us, so we need never suffer under the fear of not having what we need. However, our unbelief may torment us nonetheless.

It is in this second category that God works to grow us. When we meet a place of suffering, we would do well to see it as an invitation into more. The Father's heart is to upgrade us in that situation. As we cooperate with Him, we step into the invitation to live increasingly according to a conviction of the things not seen.

This process is what the book of Hebrews refers to as "the discipline of the Lord" (Hebrews 12:5). Often the discipline of the Lord is portrayed as God's punishment for our poor choices. That is not the idea at all. In context, we see that the discipline of the Lord is the way the Lord works in us when we are in challenging situations we want to leave:

> Therefore, since we are surrounded by so great a cloud of witnesses, let us also lay aside every weight, and sin which clings so closely, and let us run with endurance the race that is set before us. . . . It is for discipline that you have to endure. God is treating you as sons. For what son is there whom his father does not discipline? . . . He disciplines us for our good, that we may share his holiness. For the moment all discipline seems painful rather than pleasant, but later it yields the peaceful fruit of righteousness to those who have been trained by it.
>
> Hebrews 12:1, 7, 10–11

Note the concept repeatedly connected to discipline here: *endurance*. We endure through challenging situations, learning to find a place of faith. This is training, and it is training that brings us into a place of sharing in God's holiness. This is not about punishment for poor choices. It is about making us disciples.

When I used to teach martial arts, I would have students from all levels of athleticism and background experience. One of the first things I would do was impose discipline on them. I would have them practice the basics, and I would push them to use their bodies in ways they never had before. I would take them through repetitive exercises designed to draw out of them the potential to be a martial artist. I disciplined them by creating a structure and a process that drew out what was possible.

This is the way the discipline of the Lord works in our lives. The suffering we experience and the challenging situations we go through are opportunities for the Lord to work in us a structure of faith. This process draws out our potential as believers. It yields the fruit of the righteousness the Lord has already given us. In the context of that, we begin to share in God's holiness.

What does it mean to share in God's holiness? *Holiness* does not mean "moral purity." It means "being set apart." As we grow in our faith, we are increasingly set apart from the world because our inner world is connected to a different one. Our life is "hidden with Christ in God" (Colossians 3:3). We still live on the earth, and we still look to partner with God's Kingdom here, but our preoccupation and our internal focus are on the heavenly reality. This draws out of us a stability and steadfastness that mirrors God's nature:

> Jesus Christ is the same yesterday and today and forever.
>
> Hebrews 13:8

As we are continually disciplined into a life of faith, we begin to partake in the unchanging nature of God. We begin to become immovable, just like He is. God is described as immutable—unchanging—meaning He does not change in different situations. This does not mean He is always identical from one moment to the next. Scripture portrays God as having emotions and living in connection to the things that are happening at any given moment.

It means God's experience of life is never changed by the situations happening around Him. He does not panic or get nervous when problems arise. He does not worry about whether the angels will be able to hold back Satan's forces. He is not overwhelmed with all the work there is to be done down here on earth. No, His inner state is stable. He is enjoying rest and peace and joy in every moment. He loves being God and is confident in His ability to be God in every possible situation. Nothing ever gets under His skin or ruins His day.

This immutability is meant to be our inheritance. We are meant to partake in this same unchanging nature and to begin to experience life this same way.

It is only in the context of our challenges that we have the opportunity to live out this facet of God's personality. Jesus did the same:

> For it was fitting that he, for whom and by whom all things exist, in bringing many sons to glory, should make the founder of their salvation perfect through suffering.
>
> Hebrews 2:10

For a long time, this verse confused me, as it indicates Jesus was only made perfect through suffering—which implies He was not perfect before He suffered. In what sense was that the case? We know He was sinless before He suffered, so it was not about moral perfection, then. It was about being a perfect representation of God. The unchanging nature of God can only be demonstrated in the face of resistance or opposition. To manifest a complete picture of God, Jesus had to demonstrate that God is not moved or changed by suffering.

This is an invitation to us, as well. God's immutability is a reality in which we can partake. We do not need to view suffering or challenge as an enemy. Many of us try to push our lives into a place where nothing opposes or resists us. Sometimes we think our challenges are an indication of weak faith. But I believe our suffering is another opportunity for us to demonstrate the nature of God—just as much as moving in the miraculous, demonstrating God's mercy to the poor or preaching the Gospel are. Our primary goal is not to escape resistance. Our primary goal is to reveal God within it.

Every time the enemy sends his will into our lives, he takes a risk. He is trying to push us off our stability, to get us to lose control of our inner world and to begin to spin out of control. Each time he does that, however, he chances our stepping into the nature of God that lives above the challenges he sends our way. As we learn to receive the Lord's discipline and manifest His unchanging nature, we begin to reveal God through the very things the enemy sends into our lives. Whether what is happening had its start in God's heart or not, we demonstrate and reveal God in it. It is as Paul says:

> But we have this treasure in jars of clay, to show that the surpassing power belongs to God and not to us. We are afflicted in every way, but not crushed; perplexed, but not driven to despair; persecuted, but not forsaken; struck down, but not destroyed; always carrying in the body the death of Jesus, so that the life of Jesus may also be manifested in our bodies. For we who live are always being given over to death for Jesus' sake, so that the life of Jesus also may be manifested in our mortal flesh. So death is at work in us, but life in you.
>
> Since we have the same spirit of faith according to what has been written, "I believed, and so I spoke," we also believe, and so we also speak, knowing that he who raised the Lord Jesus will raise us also with Jesus and bring us with you into his presence. For it is all for your sake, so that as grace extends to more and more people it may increase thanksgiving, to the glory of God.
>
> So we do not lose heart. Though our outer self is wasting away, our inner self is being renewed day by day. For this light momentary affliction is preparing for us an eternal weight of glory beyond all comparison, as we look not to the things that are seen but to the things that are unseen. For the things that are seen are transient, but the things that are unseen are eternal.
>
> 2 Corinthians 4:7–18

THINKING LIKE JESUS

- Faith is not about confidence or belief. It is the accurate perception of spiritual realities.
- As we live in faith, our life flows from an inner connection to God, not from an outer connection to things in the physical world.
- Every challenge or suffering we endure in life is an opportunity for us to enter deeper into a life of faith and of living from the truth.

11

Be His Face

I t is Sunday evening and the eleven remaining disciples are huddled together, terrified. Their best friend and hero has just gone from being Jerusalem's most popular teacher to being murdered and buried, and in less than a week. The disciples know those same Jews are out there and will stop at nothing to put down this movement Jesus started.

Jesus had been controversial, sure. But He was just so . . . well, *good*. The idea that someone would want to take the life of a man who brought healing and help to the poor, the broken and the helpless was unthinkable. But it happened. And not only had there been a price on Jesus' head, but there was probably one on the heads of Peter, James, John and the others, as well.

During the Passover, Jerusalem has been packed. It would not be safe to try to make a run for it and head back to Galilee, and the Pharisees might be looking for them there anyway. What option is there? Hide . . . hunker down until the festivities pass. Then, in a few days, sneak out of town after all the attention dies down.

That is exactly what they did. They pulled the window shades, barred the doors and did everything possible to stay out of sight.

So here we have eleven of the most confused, terrified men you can imagine. Just days before, their wildest dreams were coming true. Now all of that has been dashed on the rocks of despair and terror.

As they huddle in the darkness, one glances to the side and sees a shape that was not there a moment earlier. It moves, and panic erupts in the group. Fear grips each of them, as some are caught frozen and others jump and scream with fright. Immediately, a voice tries to calm them, but only after amplifying the chaos first. Eventually, the words settle in: "It's okay . . . be at peace . . . calm down . . ."

"Here, look," the voice continues. The unknown Person stretches out His arms to reveal deep scarring on His hands, then brushes aside His garment to reveal a similar recovered wound in His side.

Could it be? How? They recalled the rumors—but could it be possible? Didn't John say he watched Him die? But this . . . this is Jesus. Jesus! He is back!

The joy and glory of that moment could only be understood by the eleven who shared it. The helplessness that had become the disciples' reality melted away and was replaced by laughter and rejoicing. They whooped and shouted, crying out, "This is amazing, Jesus! You not only have defeated sickness, but You beat death—Your own death! This changes everything!"

For a long time, the eleven alternated between looking at Him and letting the unbelievable reality set in and being overcome with laughter and joy at the return of the most important Person in the world to them.

Eventually, Jesus collected their attention. "All right, everybody," He said. "I've got some good news for you. I'm now going to send you out with My peace and My wholeness. As the Father has sent Me, even so I am sending you."

Those words spun in the disciples' minds. As the Father sent Jesus, He was sending them the same way? But they had seen how the Father sent Jesus the last three years. He sent Jesus to be His face. To represent Him. To be the visible image of the invisible God. To be able to say, "If you've seen Me, you've seen the Father." That was the way He was sending them, too?

While the implications of this worked its way through their minds, Jesus continued.

"I know you guys need some help," He said. "You see, I came as God in a human body. You have the body, but you need God. Receive the Holy Spirit . . ."

And He breathed on them, just as His Father had breathed into Adam so many years ago. The disciples inhaled a deep breath as the very Spirit of God made His home in them. The same Holy Spirit that had empowered all the incredible things they had seen was now living in them, empowering them. They were now sent with His empowering to represent their victorious King.

The Commission

The disciples were sent with the commission the Church has carried for the last two thousand years. In the gospels of Matthew, Mark and Luke, it is represented missionally, but John captures it relationally: "As the Father has sent me, even so I am sending you."

This is our call. This is our charge. To be the visible image of the invisible Jesus. To be able to say, "If you've seen me, you've seen the Lord." It is a calling none of us lives out perfectly, but it is what we are called to nonetheless. Jesus came not only to

: a new identity and to reclaim this world from the devil,
so to give us a clear picture of what the original design
looks like. He is the picture of what we were always meant to
be and what we truly are in Him.

Claims like that seem extraordinary, and they are. I agree with
that assessment. To believe them requires faith. This concept
stretches me! Nevertheless, God has designed us and called us
to live out of a union with Him. Jesus is the Vine; we are the
branches. We are connected to Him, and our life flows from
Him. We are an extension of who He is, bearing that fruit in the
world. We are more literally than metaphorically the Body of
Christ. Jesus still has a body on this earth; it is in you and me.

It is, of course, only this kind of calling that could restore
to us what Adam and Eve lost in the Garden. We were created
to bear the image and likeness of God, to create a recognition
of who He is through who we are. This calling is a restoration
to that starting point. We now are called to be the image and
likeness of the risen Christ. This is our charge. This is our
calling, and the Gospel of Jesus Christ is what gets us there.

In this Gospel is our righteousness. After Adam and Eve
turned away from God and, through their choice, all of humanity was marred by the indwelling presence of sin, Jesus came to
die and resurrect all who place their faith in Him. In Him, we are
born again as a new creation, free from sin. We are new, clean,
pure. We are what God always intended us to be, and we are
growing into seeing ourselves and our lives through this story.

In this Gospel is our New Covenant of grace. After the Israelites turned away from the invitation to be priests and to
have direct access to God, the Law put a covenant of separation between God and man. Jesus came and offered Himself
for our forgiveness as the required sacrifice under the Law and
introduced a New Covenant that guarantees there will never

again be distance or separation between those who follow Jesus and the Father.

In this Gospel is the Kingdom of God. After Satan hijacked the authority God granted to Adam and Eve and became the god of this world, Jesus came as a challenging King. Through His death and resurrection, He overthrew the rule of the enemy and procured authority on the earth again. Under His authority, we are commissioned to bring this world into alignment with the will of the Father. God has poured out the Holy Spirit upon the Church so that every enemy of Jesus becomes subject to His rulership.

This is our Gospel, our Good News. It is a reality we are invited into, and it can be the story of the rest of our lives. Jesus has given us glorious good news, and He invites us to live so fully in this good news that, through us, He can shine His light into the darkness of the world.

Let us now lay aside every distraction and every misconception that holds us back from this glorious truth, and let us run after this great vision. Let us run with perseverance and courage this road, all the while looking to Jesus—our great champion and hero—the One who writes His faith upon us and forges it in times of great authority and in times of painful suffering. He is our forerunner and our model, and this great vision empowered Him to press through the shame and degradation of crucifixion. He is now victorious. Our conquering King, seated on a throne in heaven and having poured out the promised Holy Spirit, now looks to His Church to continue what He started.

The Gospel

A few years ago, I took a group of our local School of Kingdom Ministry graduates on a short mission trip to Mexico a few weeks after graduation. It was a capstone of our one-year journey together. We saw many incredible things happen as we ministered the love and power of Jesus, both in churches and through several outreaches.

One of the days we were there, as a unique outreach opportunity, we drove into the mountains of central Mexico to spend time ministering to an unreached indigenous people group. This was a tribal people, complete with witchdoctors. Talk about an out-of-the-normal experience! I was honored and humbled that we could minister to these people, and before we went, I looked forward to what the Lord would do.

The day before we were to minister to them, I met with some of our team members who were in the process of moving to this area of Mexico to be missionaries. I asked them what would be the most beneficial thing we could do there, since they were the ones who would be there for the long haul. I wanted the biggest win for them.

The young couple shared with me that local churches had built a good relationship with this tribe, but there was not much in terms of the Gospel. The tribe had learned to be excited about Jesus, but they did not know why. It was a matter of culture they had picked up from their new friends.

The next day, we took the long journey up into the mountains. When we arrived, we made sandwiches and served everyone food. We then gathered in groups and shared with the members of the tribe.

As the team leader, I was asked to share with the largest group, about sixty women ranging from young mothers to the elderly. Standing before them and sharing the Gospel was one of the highest honors of my life.

I said to them, "I am so excited to be here with you today. You are a deeply spiritual people and are in touch with the spiritual world. I think this is something we can learn from you. My people have forgotten the truth of the spiritual world, but you know it well.

"I am here today because I want to share a truth about the spiritual world. I want to talk about the Most High God, the most powerful God there is over all the gods there are. That God sees us and loves us. He looked down and saw that we are not what we could be. Don't we all follow the wrong way sometimes? We are selfish in our hearts and look out for ourselves instead of others.

"So, that Most High God came down and became a man named Jesus. He was born as a baby and became a little boy"—at this point, I smiled and poked a young boy who was present with his mom—"and He grew up to be a man. He showed us the true way to live. He showed us how to love and what we can be.

"Because He was the Most High God, He also was powerful. He drove out evil spirits, and He healed all the sick. He came to fix the broken world. Then He died, but He was so powerful, He overthrew death and came back to life.

"Now, because He died and came back to life, He does not have to be a body. He comes to live inside our hearts when we believe in Him. When He does, He makes us what we are supposed to be, and He empowers us to live the right way. He lives in me right now, and He can live in you, too.

"To prove that all of this is true, that the Most High God can live in you if you trust Him, I'm going to heal the sick here. It is not me healing the sick, but Jesus in me who will heal the sick. Who here needs healing?"

At that point, one younger woman toward the front cautiously raised her hand.

I reiterated, "Now, to demonstrate to you that the Most High God lives in me and He can live in you, too, if you ask Him to, I'm going to pray for her, and she will be healed."

I stepped forward and asked the woman what was wrong. She seemed embarrassed and shied away from telling me. I thought, *What? I just double-guaranteed this woman's healing to prove the Gospel to this tribal people, and she's not cooperating?* I panicked inside for a second, then reminded myself Jesus is bigger than all of this.

"No problem," I continued, and I put my hand on her shoulder. Then I prayed, "I command all sickness and pain to leave you right now, in Jesus' name. Be healed."

I stepped back and asked the woman how she felt as I motioned for the translator to give her the microphone.

"It's gone," she said.

As soon as those words landed in the small crowd, about six other hands shot up of people who needed healing. My team jumped in, and we spent almost an hour praying for people as they were healed of all kinds of conditions. Migraines were broken off. Stomach issues were healed. Deaf ears popped open. Healing after healing rippled through the crowd as a testimony of the lordship of Jesus and the truth of His Gospel. Except for one boy who had an extreme palsy, everyone we prayed for was completely healed. I would estimate at least twelve to twenty people were healed that day.

I wish I could tell you that after that, I made a call for salvation and the whole group dedicated themselves to Jesus. But in the chaos of everything, we did not have a chance to do it. Jesus has continued His work in that tribe, though. As I write this, it is closing in on four years since that day, and the missionaries have continued to minister to the people. The tribe has experienced their first baptism, and many have placed their faith in Jesus. In fact, the dynamic is no longer one of "unreached people group" as much as "persecuted Church," since the village leaders at times threaten to claim their land or homes for following Jesus. Despite this, the family of believers in that tribe continues to grow. I recently learned a couple from the tribe has begun to attend Bible training school to be able to minister more effectively to their people.

On the van ride back to the hostel where we were staying that day, we all shared the incredible stories of what we saw Jesus do as we prayed. I thought, *This is amazing! This was a day straight out of the book of Acts. Who gets to do this?*

Not every day of my life looks like that, but that is not the only story I can tell that feels like it belongs in the Bible. In fact, stories like this are becoming more and more the norm for me.

None of us is meant for a normal life. God has been sealed inside our very humanity. There is nothing normal about us left. Set aside how you see yourself and who the world may say you are—God's view of you is truth. Embrace His definition of you, and discover the power and the impact of who God has made you to be and what happens when He empowers the new creation He has made you in Christ.

Appendix

Gospel Summary

This appendix is meant to provide a simple summary of the three strands of the Gospel—identity, destiny and relationship—and how they flow throughout Scripture.

	Identity	Destiny	Relationship
Original Design	Mankind created in the image and likeness of God	Mankind given dominion over the earth	Intimate relationship between God and mankind
Problems Introduced at the Fall	Image of God fractured and broken	Dominion given over to Satan	God and mankind estranged and separated by a covenant (the Law) to keep them apart
Lost State	Sinful nature	Satan is the god of this world	Need for forgiveness; under the wrath of God
Jesus' Example	The visible image of the invisible God	The strongman who binds Satan and drives him out	Father-Son relationship with God

Gospel Solution	We are crucified and resurrected with Jesus; our sinful nature is killed, and we are born again as a new creation	Jesus triumphs over the powers of darkness and reclaims all authority on the earth; we are sent out under His commissioning	Jesus is offered as the payment required by the Law for the whole world; He allows us to know God as Father
Gospel Language	*Righteousness by faith*, meaning we are right in our being by trusting what Jesus did for us	*Kingdom of God*, meaning God's active rule on the earth	*New Covenant of grace*, meaning a new relationship in which Jesus will never leave us or forsake us

Notes

Chapter 2: The Gospel I Thought I Knew

1. Scot McKnight, "Jesus vs. Paul," *Christianity Today*, December 3, 2010, http://www.christianitytoday.com/ct/2010/december/9.25.html.

Chapter 4: The True Gospel

1. Edwin H. Friedman, *A Failure of Nerve: Leadership in the Age of the Quick Fix* (New York: Seabury Books, 2007), 36.

Chapter 6: A Tale of Two Natures

1. In context, "flesh and blood" in this passage refers to the relationships we have with people around us. One might argue Paul is referring to something different with his use of the term "flesh" here, but I would suggest he is using the term the same way he uses it every other time: to describe the natural world in which we live.

2. The word Paul chooses here is the Greek word (*metamorphoo*), meaning "transfigured." It is the same word used in two accounts of the Transfiguration. The final use of the word in Scripture is found in 2 Corinthians 3:18, where Paul discusses similar ideas from a slightly different angle.

Chapter 7: What about Forgiveness?

1. In Romans 4, we learn God counted Abraham's faith as righteousness— in other words, that God saw Abraham's faith and treated him as if he were righteous, even though he was not. We are in a different situation than Abraham was because we have been *made* righteous by faith. That being the case,

we ought to have much more confidence in our access to relationship with the Father.

2. This was sound teaching at the time. Jesus did not create the New Covenant until His death at the cross, so John the Baptist was teaching the truth that applied at the time.

3. Another Scripture we could insert here is Luke 24:47. There is apparently some disagreement as to how exactly this should be translated, though, so this Scripture is less clear on this point.

4. We can, however, still need to *receive* forgiveness in areas of our lives that go awry because of the effects of sin. Sin is not without consequence, but God is not the one sending consequences into our lives. The consequences come from reaping the sin that we (or others) sow. Even in this, the Lord has provided the means to receive His grace and be restored to wholeness.

Chapter 8: The Gospel of the Kingdom

1. *Demonized* is a term many scholars believe more accurately depicts the experience of those described in Scripture than the term *demon possession*. The idea conveyed in the original language is more along the lines of "someone afflicted by demons" than "someone owned by demons."

2. I believe a further implication is that, as the Church continues in its work, the Spirit will be poured out more and more until He is poured out on "all flesh" (Acts 2:17), in complete fulfillment of the Joel 2 prophecy that started to be fulfilled in Acts 2.

3. We often label a quick or intuitive learner as someone who is gifted.

Chapter 9: Christ in Us

1. Jocelin, *The Life and Acts of St. Patrick*, trans. Edmund L. Swift, 1809, as quoted by Our Lady of the Rosary Library, "Resurrection Miracles Performed by Saint Patrick, Apostle of Ireland," https://www.olrl.org/lives/patrick.shtml.

2. As quoted by EWTN, "Lorica of Saint Patrick," https://www.ewtn.com/Devotionals/prayers/patrick.htm.

3. Blue Letter Bible, "H1823—*dĕmuwth*," https://www.blueletterbible.org/lang/Lexicon/Lexicon.cfm?strongs=H1823&t=KJV.

4. If you want to explore this idea further, 1 Corinthians 2 has much more to say on this subject.

5. From what I have read, some of the language is lost in translation, and these Church fathers are making the same point I am in the language that was used in their day. They are not asserting we are independent deities but rather that we are joined with and partake of Christ in such a way that we can experience God's deity and live from that place.

While in the process of obtaining a Ph.D. in theoretical quantum physics, **Putty Putman** ran headlong into the power and reality of the Holy Spirit during a supernatural encounter in China. Following the leading of Jesus to sell everything he had to purchase the Pearl of Great Price, Putty terminated a successful career in physics to pursue a life of learning, leading and training others to move in the power of the Holy Spirit.

Putty is on the senior leadership team of the Vineyard Church of Central Illinois, co-leads its preaching team and oversees the School of Kingdom Ministry, a supernatural training and discipleship school hosted by local churches across the country and around the world. A gifted communicator and passionate equipper, Putty loves to see people grow in the conviction of who they are in Christ and be released to live a naturally supernatural lifestyle empowered by the Holy Spirit.

Putty lives in Champaign, Illinois, with his wife, Brittany, and three children. For more information, visit:

www.thevineyardchurch.us
www.schoolofkingdomministry.org
www.facebook.com/puttyputman

Be who God made you

school of KINGDOM MINISTRY

Join thousands of believers around the world on a journey of discovering who you are in Christ and being released to move in the power of the Holy Spirit. **The School of Kingdom Ministry** is hosted at local churches and partners with pastors and leaders to bring supernatural discipleship to your church, family and community.

Join the family and take the journey of discovering the life God has for us all!

SCHOOLOFKINGDOMMINISTRY.ORG